MY SON, YO-YO

By Marina Ma

As Told to John A. Rallo

The Chinese University Press

My Son, Yo-Yo

by Marina Ma, as told to John A. Rallo

ISBN 962–201–640–5

First edition 1995
Second printing 1996
Third printing 2000
Fourth printing 2002

THE CHINESE UNIVERSITY PRESS
The Chinese University of Hong Kong
Sha Tin, N. T., Hong Kong
Fax: +852 2603 6692
　　 +852 2603 7355
E-mail: cup@cuhk.edu.hk
Web-site: www.chineseupress.com

Printed in Hong Kong

Dedicated
to the Memory of
Dr. Hiao-Tsiun Ma
Founder of
THE CHILDREN'S ORCHESTRA
New York, Paris, Taipei

Grateful acknowledgment is made to
Catherine R. Rallo
for her invaluable assistance
in the preparation of the manuscript

Contents

Appendices

Music in our hearts
is the Springtime of life

Introduction

"Musical superstars seem to have something in common. A surprisingly large number came from musical or theatrical families and were exposed to music from babyhood. Their talent showed up early, and most of them made their first public appearance at an alarmingly early age. From the beginning most of them seemed to have a kind of personality and projection that, coupled to their markedly superior talent, immediately set them apart from their colleagues. They had that mysterious factor X, the ingredient that enabled them to generate frenzy in the audience."

Harold C. Schonberg, *The Glorious Ones*[1]

Friendship between our two families dates back to the Fall of 1965, when both Dr. Hiao-Tsiun Ma and I held positions at the École Française in Manhattan, he as music director, and I as administrative director-designate. During that period, his two children, Yo-Yo and Yeou-Cheng, were principal players in the Children's String Orchestra. My own two sons, Christopher and John-Peter, taught by Dr. Ma, were members of that Orchestra.

It had always been Dr. Ma's belief that music, like any language, was best learned by children at a very young age. "Music," he said, "changes the way of life of the child and orchestra playing improves him. Children learn to think better when they make music together; they no longer play mere notes, they make music."

His dream of children playing good music became a reality when,

---

1. Harold C. Schonberg, *The Glorious Ones* (Times Books, New York: Random House, 1985), p. xii.

in the short span of a few years, he founded and directed The Children's Orchestra in New York, and later in Paris and in Taiwan.

As our friendship grew, so did the fame of one tiny member of the orchestra: his son, Yo-Yo. Today, he enjoys international renown, while his parents have gloated over the realization of their dreams.

Several years ago, I encouraged Mrs. Ma to put into writing some episodes of her son's life. "You are the only one who can do it," I told her. "Who else knows Yo-Yo more intimately than you?" His story must be told. Do it now, while the details are still vivid in your mind."

Marina Ma agreed, but she was too modest, even reluctant to undertake the task.

"You know Yo-Yo," she said. "Why don't you write the story yourself?"

At that point, the matter was laid to rest.

Two years later, fate struck. Dr. Ma suffered an irreversible stroke. Since he was no longer able to talk and without hope of ever recovering, I prevailed upon Mrs. Ma not to put off writing her son's story while there was still time for her to tell it. Her husband's unexpected illness convinced her.

On 12 September 1990, my wife and I went to the Mas' apartment in Manhattan to share reminiscences of her early family life.

*   *   *

Marina Ma was there to greet us as the elevator stopped on the fifth floor. "So glad to see you," she said. "Please, you go in first. I'll hold the door for you."

With that simple but warm welcome, we went inside the apartment.

Before making ourselves comfortable, Mrs. Ma ushered us directly to her husband's bedside.

"Daddy," she called out in a soft voice, "the Rallos are here. They've come to see you."

He turned his head and stared at me with languid eyes, raising his right arm, the only part of his body over which he had some control. I reached out for his hand and grasped it.

"You look well, *mon ami*," I said. "Much better than the last time I saw you."

He blinked his eyes to express appreciation for my visit. A moment of silence. But in that silence we felt the warmth of friendship. A clasp of hands communicated our unspoken feelings. The body has a language of its own.

"We mustn't tire him," Mrs. Ma said, as she adjusted a pillow under his head and pulled up a blanket to his chest. Then, stroking his forehead gently, she added, "We'll come back later, Daddy."

While my wife buried her nose in a book, Mrs. Ma and I settled in the living room near a large window. Below, the street level re-echoed with the usual cacophony of sounds: the screeching of automobiles, the screaming of ambulance and police sirens, the ceaseless honking of horns — all the dissonant sounds of a busy city in motion.

Oblivious to the noise, Mrs. Ma turned her thoughts inward, recalling earlier years. As she spoke, she moved her head slightly in the direction of her husband's bedroom, where he lay immobile. "At least he has a partial view of the sky from his window, and at night, when he can't sleep, he can look at the stars. I keep his window closed most of the time; the air pollution is so bad, to say nothing of the exhaust fumes from buses and automobiles."

Again she glanced toward the bedroom from which floated soft strains of Mozart and Bach. Her eyes moistened and a lump knotted in her throat.

She changed the subject.

"You can't imagine how much I appreciate your coming here for my story, Dr. Rallo. You have known my children all these years and have watched them grow up…"

We still addressed each other in the formal language of the old order using titles and last names, even though our two families have been friends for more than a generation.

Marina Ma began her story, highlighting Yo-Yo's childhood, a compelling story of love, devotion and sacrifices told in a simple way.

John A. Rallo
Connecticut, August 1994

1. A Child Prodigy Is Born

As soon as Marina opened the entrance door, Grandma shuffled past in. It was the second Thursday of the month and she had come for her customary visit. She didn't say anything as she passed in front of her daughter-in-law but greeted her warmly with an affectionate bow of her head and went straight to a wicker chair in front of the piano. She plunked herself down and began rubbing her feet. They hurt. They always hurt after walking. Little Yeou-Cheng lost no time in jumping on her lap and giving her a big hug. She loved Grandma so much. Then the usual ritual began, with Grandma putting a severe look on her face.

"Has my little girl been good?"

"Oh, yes, Grandma. I've been very good. Ask Mommy."

"No need of that, child. I believe you."

Then she dug into her pocket and pulled out a tangerine.

"See what I've brought you? Fresh fruit is the best thing for you."

Yeou-Cheng thanked her with a kiss and headed for the kitchen to feast on the tangerine, which Grandma had peeled for her.

Grandma then turned to Marina. "My, how our little girl has grown! And in the next breath she added, "It's time you had a second child."

Her tone was matriarchal.

"Other couples have a baby every other year," she continued, "it's now more than two years since Yeou-Cheng was born."

Marina was not surprised by what she heard; she had heard the same words over and over again so many times before. That too had become a ritual.

Marina could well sympathize with her mother-in-law's eagerness

Grandmother holding Yeou-Cheng, "It's time you had another child."

for another child; it was traditional among Chinese families to have several children. And she knew that her mother-in-law hoped for a baby boy to carry the family name.

Marina looked at her in-law's lined face and felt compassion, but her constant harping on a second child was beginning to wear thin; it was the only point of unspoken friction between the two. The old woman meant well; Marina knew that; she knew that her mother-in-law was steeped in an age-old tradition and that she did not fully realize the poor financial condition the young couple found itself in. It was utter folly to even think of adding another member to the family. Her husband, Dr. Hiao-Tsiun Ma, was a hard worker, but his meagre income was insufficient to provide for the barest necessities. France was experiencing dire economic problems and there was little work to be had. And even then whatever work might be available was given to French citizens and not to foreigners.

Grandma Chu Pou sat silently in her chair.

"Would you like a cup of tea?" Marina asked. "It's jasmine flavoured, the kind you always drink."

She accepted the tea ceremoniously, and the two chatted about their mutual relatives and conditions back in China. Time dragged.

When she had finished her tea, Grandma called Yeou-Cheng to come to kiss her good-bye.

As Marina opened the door for her, Grandma gave her a benevolent, motherly look, accompanied by a sigh. "It's time you had another child." Then she disappeared in the narrow, dark corridor that led to the stairs.

Grandma was not the only one to encourage her to have a second child. The piano teacher, who had been giving Yeou-Cheng free lessons and knew of her financial condition, also voiced a similar thought. Given the Mas' unusual background in music and Yeou-Cheng's extraordinary talent, she rationalized that they should not miss the chance of bringing another gifted child into the world. She was firmly convinced that a solution would be found.

One day, when Marina went to pick up her daughter after her music lesson, the teacher took her aside. "Your daughter is a brilliant musician," she began, "I'm sure you're aware of that. There's no doubt

Mmm… I wonder what mother is knitting.

in my mind that she inherits this talent from you and your husband.... It's in her genes."

Marina held back her embarrassment. She just smiled. What could she say? If nature had provided this gift, then so be it. She was merely the vessel that brought her into the world. She could take no credit for that.

"Mrs. Ma," the teacher continued, "what I'm trying to tell you is that I think it is a great pity that you don't plan on having another child."

The words struck home. Had the teacher been talking with the grandmother, she wondered. But that was impossible. The two women had never met.

"And where would I put another child," Marina blurted out, not knowing what else to say.

"Why," the teacher quipped making light of the situation, "you can always find room on top the piano!"

They both burst out in nervous laughter.

But Marina did not laugh a few days later when she recounted the episode to one of her closest friends.

"I think it's a very bad idea," her friend said, "the teacher had no right telling you that. You have neither the money nor the room. How on earth are you going to provide for another child? You should be satisfied with just raising Yeou-Cheng."

Seeing that Marina was quite disturbed about the whole matter and as an afterthought she added, "At least for the time being..."

Neither the Grandmother nor the teacher offered Marina any real comfort, but she felt that her friend had a better understanding of the situation. When she discussed the matter with her husband, he made it quite clear that Marina should not be talking about such personal matters with her friends. It was none of their business. Then he confessed that he too had been thinking about having another child and made no bones about it. His sister had died recently and a new baby would help brighten up his mother's spirit during this period of mourning. Hiao-Tsiun's mind had been made up. "Marina," he said to his wife, "my mother and the teacher are absolutely right. I've given the matter a lot of consideration. It's not good for us to have just the one child..." He was venting his own feelings. He yearned to have a son who would continue the family name, for he adhered strictly to the codified tradition instilled in him from early childhood.

Marina stood there, words frozen on her lips. Hiao-Tsiun paced up and down as he usually did when in thought. Suddenly he stopped in front of his wife and looked straight at her. "We'll manage, we'll manage," he repeated.

Marina understood; she well read the determination in his eyes. There was nothing more to be said. Hiao-Tsiun smiled a broad smile, his black eyes twinkling behind his thick, silver-rimmed glasses.

On 7 October 1955, a seven-and-a-half pound baby boy was born in Paris. He was given the Christian name Ernest and the Chinese name "Yo," which means friend. "Ma," the family's generational character signifies "horse"; "Yo Ma" translates into "Friendly Horse."

"Yo," however, did not sound musical enough to the Mas' ears, so they added another "Yo" rendering the name more melodious. "Yo-Yo" rolled easily on the tongue.

Marina greatly worried throughout her pregnancy; she did not know how they were going to meet the extra expenses, where they were going to find room in their tight quarters, and for how much longer her husband's stipend was going to hold out. These thoughts were constantly on her mind; she felt helpless and guilty. Guilty for not

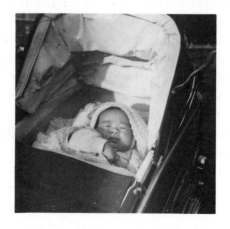

Peaceful slumber.

having put up stronger resistance to her husband; for having failed to make him see the predicament he was plunging them into. Even as the labour pains started, she was convinced the timing had been all wrong. But when she heard the first cry from her new-born, she realized how mistaken she had been; how she too had subconsciously submerged her feelings for another child. She realized that all the excuses she had made and all the denials were but a cover-up for her true feelings. As she looked at Yo-Yo's round face and full cheeks, she muttered to herself, "Marina, Marina, what a fortunate woman you are!"

Days later, as she cuddled her baby in her arms, she experienced a calming effect she had not felt since the birth of Yeou-Cheng, four years earlier, on 28 July 1951. She called her husband, "Look, Look! Yo-Yo's eyes are open and they're gazing straight at the light."

Hiao-Tsiun was amused by what must have sounded to him like a

A mother's pride.

Yo-Yo at the age of nine months.

mother's naïve remark. Maybe he even guessed his wife's secret hope that their child would be as talented as Yeou-Cheng.

"Yes," he agreed, not wishing to dispel her happy mood. He bent down for a closer look and was amazed to see that Yo-Yo's eyes were indeed focused on the light.

Was Marina deluding herself? Was it wishful thinking on her part to read more into that steady gaze? Would that small piece of flesh whose two eyes were staring straight at the light make their dreams come true?

Marina kissed her boy's soft cheek and wondered as tears filled her eyes.

2. Bitter Cold It Was

My Grandmother
Bound feet, symbol of bondage from childhood;
I loved to tease her and hide her shoes.
How could I have known the pain endured
And forgotten by her little bound feet?

Yeou-Cheng

The year Yo-Yo was born was replete with anxiety for the Mas. The small stipend Dr. Ma received as a graduate student at the University of Paris Conservatory of Music, was barely enough to feed his family. As for rental money, he could not afford to pay more than what he did for the one-room in the old, walk-up building subsidized by the University. To add to their misery, Winter arrived earlier than usual. In fact, it was the coldest Winter Parisians could remember.

The wind, light at first, stripped whatever leaves clung desperately to the branches. Then, as the wind howled and increased in intensity, it sucked them off in a wild, aimless direction until they fell on the ground to be swept away once again. The days grew shorter and the rays of the sun lost their cold glimmer.

Huddled in their heatless room, with temperatures below freezing point, the Mas worried about their future. Their meagre savings were practically exhausted; yet they had to find warmer quarters. An icy room was no place for a baby.

Tired and overworked as he was, Dr. Ma took on more private students for extra earnings. This enabled him to rent a hotel room for his wife and child. There, they would be warmer, he thought.

He was wrong.

France was still undergoing its slow, painful recovery from the Second World War and her eventual defeat by the Vietminh at the Battle of Dien-Bien-Phu in 1954, during the Indo-China War. Stringent economic measures were still in effect throughout the nation.

The hotel management, under pressure to hold down maintenance costs, shut off all heat during the night. The rooms turned ice-cold.

One especially frigid night, Marina woke up with a start. Had she heard a noise in her sleep or had anxiety played with her imagination? She wasn't sure.

In spite of the street clothes she was wearing in bed for added warmth, the freezing cold had penetrated her body. She sat up. For a fleeting moment her mother's instinct warned that something was terribly wrong with her baby. She panicked. Quietly she crept to his side. She felt his body. It was ice. She picked him up and cradled him in her arms, praying with wordless prayers that the heat of her own body would somehow flow into that tiny infant, feeding him warmth.

A thousand anxieties assailed her as she held him closer to her bosom. She found herself alone, facing what might be an inevitable ending. She, who had shown so much courage in other circumstances, wished her husband were at her side. He'd know what else to do. But she was alone.

"Please, oh please, don't let anything happen to my baby," she sobbed.

Then, as if her prayer had been answered, she saw the colour return to Yo-Yo's cheeks.

The night of dread gave way to hope.

Had they been back in that one-room apartment, her child surely would not have lived through the night. For that much she was thankful.

Fortunately, Marina was a survivor. From early childhood in Hong Kong, she had learned to stand up on her own. Even her mother-in-law could not lend her a helping hand since she had enough to do caring for Hiao-Tsiun and Yeou-Cheng. Besides, had she wanted to, she could not walk the short distance to the hotel: every step she took was agony, for she was a victim of the ancient Chinese custom (binding), which deformed her feet.

Long ago, the Chinese male had invented a myth to prevent his mate from committing infidelity. At birth, a baby girl's feet were tightly bound to stunt their growth. As a result, the adult woman experienced such excruciating pain that she walked with a mincing gait that was highly prized by the male-dominated society. In reality, it was just a pretext for keeping a woman close to home.

Somehow they survived the Winter. When the air turned warm, the Mas felt as if they had left Purgatory and entered the gates of Heaven. The family was together once more, ready to face whatever lay ahead. Having found their way out of the dark tunnel, they took each day as it came.

Marina and her husband had gone to Paris to fulfill their dreams and to further their musical studies. Their children were born there. Yet they had a longing nostalgia to return to their native China. Hiao-Tsiun often confessed that he dreamed of going back to teach as soon as the political situation would allow.

Marina and Yeou-Cheng; "Do I dare dream?"

"Sheer folly: returning so soon would be a big mistake," she told him.

Then she read the determination on his face. How well she read that opaque look.

"But if you insist…" she added as an afterthought, trying a different maneuver. "There's another consideration that you must take into account. Have you forgotten Yeou-Cheng? She is already showing such great promise as a pianist. Would it be fair to interrupt her lessons?"

Night after night, husband and wife spent hours debating what to do. Though making hard decisions had never fazed Hiao-Tsiun, the new dilemma put his shoulders against a wall. The thousands of music sheets with the orchestral arrangements he had made tailored to the talent of each member of a still non-existent children's orchestra were destined to continue piling up in drawers and in dark corners of the room. He had envisioned children learning to "make music" according to his own methodology and an audience seeing them with new eyes and listening to them with new ears.

All those dreams would have to be laid aside for now. Their daughter's future came first. His personal ambitions had to wait.

Four-year old Yeou-Cheng continued with piano lessons.

On sunny days, Marina used to take both children to the Luxembourg Garden. Yeou-Cheng looked so happy helping her mother push the baby carriage. Her dark bangs just above her eyes contrasted with the green of the sweater her mother had knitted. Full of joy, she skipped and jumped like a Spring-bok. She radiated exuberance. People out for an afternoon in the beautiful surroundings stared at her childish antics, especially when she waved a stick in the air, pretending to lead an imaginary orchestra. Even students from the nearby Sorbonne took time out from their books to smile at the little conductor.

All the while Marina kept a close watch over Yo-Yo, blissfully napping in his hand-me-down carriage. Vicariously she wished she were young again to dance and sing like her daughter. It seemed such a fun thing to do.

After one such afternoon in the park, Marina returned home and found her husband there. It was unusual for him to finish work so

Mother and daughter: "Directing the Orchestra."

early. He waited patiently, while she changed her baby's wet diaper. When she finished, he called her over.

"Marina," he began holding back his enthusiasm, "a colleague informed me that a couple has moved out of our building…"

She didn't let him finish. Her mind raced. Why would anyone leave an apartment when they were so hard to find even if one had enough money? Had her husband come home early to tell her that? Or had the couple been forced to move out because their rent was being raised?

"What has that got to do with us?" she asked, fearing that their rent also would be increased.

"You just don't understand. You know that I have attended the Sorbonne and got my Ph.D. in musicology from the University of Paris."

Still puzzled, she nodded.

"Well, I've applied for the larger quarters vacated by the couple. It's our lucky day.

For Marina, that meant higher rent.

"I'm sure they'll let us have it," he added philosophically. "After all,

dédiées à ma fille Yeou-Cheng Marie-Thérèse
pour son cinquième anniversaire

孟姜女四季變奏曲

Variations sur un thème populaire chinois
pour violon seul

馬孝駿 作曲
H. T. Ma

孟姜女四季變奏曲①

Allegretto

Moderato

孟姜女四季變奏曲②

I think I deserve special consideration since the University owns the building."

Marina looked him straight in the eye. He was the eternal optimist, the artist, wasn't he? And artists walk with their heads in the clouds.

"As is," she reminded him, "we have a hard time making ends meet. Pray, tell me, where would you get the extra money?"

She spoke in a controlled tone, not wanting to bring him down to reality.

Hiao-Tsiun rolled his eyes, then looked at her through his thick eyeglasses.

"You'll never change, will you? Always worrying, always afraid to take chances."

She knew that his mind was made up and that he was going to have his way.

He did.

Soon after, with renewed hope and a lot of trepidation, the Mas moved from their one-room lodging into their spacious new quarters.

Two rooms!

3. A Mind of His Own

Marina had planned to breast-feed her baby. By instinct she knew that breast-feeding was good for an infant's emotional and psychological well-being. Feeling close to a mother's breast increased the sense of security. Moreover, traditionally, it was expected of her. Had not nature provided for this?

Unfortunately, Marina didn't have enough milk. She worried. But her worry was needless, for Yo-Yo took to the formula immediately. He had a lusty appetite and gulped it down to the last drop.

Eventually, the small nipple on which he sucked had become much larger from repeated immersions in boiling water. Still, Yo-Yo enjoyed the expanded nipple so much that he refused to drink when his mother replaced it with a new, small one.

Marina was assailed by all sorts of concerns when he rejected the bottle. Was something wrong with her baby? He kept crying louder and louder. Perhaps the formula was too hot. She had always been so careful in testing it. In vain she tried to force the nipple into his mouth. It was of no use. Each time Yo-Yo forcibly spat it out, driving Marina out of her wits.

"Breton, Breton," she shouted at him. "You're just like those pig-headed men from Bretagne." The meaningless words fell on deaf ears, as Yo-Yo kept crying from hunger.

In desperation, as a last resort, she went back to the big, old nipple. To her delight, it worked. Yo-Yo began to suck ravenously.

This was Marina's first encounter with her son's stubbornness. It was not going to be her last.

From the very beginning, Yo-Yo showed that he was going to have his own way. That kind of stubbornness would continue throughout

Marina and Dr. Hiao-Tsiun Ma with Yeou-Cheng
(age 6) and Yo-Yo (age 2).

A walk in the park.

The Ma Family.

his youth, which more that once got him into trouble.

When Yo-Yo was three years old, he started piano lessons. The astounding progress he made with his prodigious fingering at the keyboard so impressed his teacher that she was sure he was no ordinary pupil.

One day, when his parents went to pick him up after his lesson, she shared her enthusiasm with them.

"Yo-Yo, why don't you play something for your parents? I'm sure they'd love to hear how well you perform."

Yo-Yo stood there, his eyes fixed on his teacher, not daring to look at his father. The child, who had always been talkative, did not say a word; he simply stood there.

Again she urged him. He didn't budge.

A happy Yo-Yo (2 years old).

Mother's little helpers; plucking a chicken (Yeou-Cheng,
7 years old; Yo-Yo, almost 3 years old).

Yeou-Cheng helps Yo-Yo celebrate his birthday.

Dr. Ma, who wasn't accustomed to such behaviour from his son, was mortified by the seeming lack of obedience. Embarrassed, he turned to him: "Yo-Yo, your teacher has asked you to play something. I'm waiting." There was a threatening tone in his voice. But Yo-Yo still refused, even though he knew his father would discipline him at home for his lack of respect.

Sensing the rising tension between father and son, the teacher spoke up in a mild, conciliatory tone: "Don't force him, Dr. Ma. Don't force him. There will be another time, I'm sure."

Brother and sister.

Mother and son in Paris.

Deep in her heart, Marina understood. She well remembered the incident of the nipple. By now she knew her son; she knew that he would not play for anyone unless he felt ready. Before sharing his music, it had to be played to his own satisfaction; it had to be perfected in his mind. Even at that early age Yo-Yo was a true performer; he would not "act" until he could say to himself, "Wow, I am ready now." He was born with that tenacious will to excel in all things that were to his liking, and though he grew up in a household where total obedience was expected, he managed to assert himself, to be defiant in spite of the consequences, which he was sure would follow.

4. Child Prodigies

"Child prodigies are still perceived as unexplained and somehow unnatural occurrences, and they have been greeted over the generations with an ambivalent mix of emotions that accompany the expectation of change: fear and wariness, mystery and myth, skepticism and contempt, awe and wonder."

David Henry Feldman, *Nature's Gambit*[2]

M arina wondered about the little signs she saw in her son and was perplexed. His behaviour did not fit into the mold generally associated with the normal development of a child. Her experience with other so-called child prodigies was limited, but in her mother's heart she knew that Yo-Yo was "different." She also knew that all parents are convinced that their children are exceptional when they show remarkable skills or behave in a manner far beyond their ages. She realized Yo-Yo was talented, but she also realized that talent alone was not sufficient to insure success in his particular field.

In *The Glorious Ones*, by Harold C. Schonberg, the well-known music critic writes:

> Certain children are born with an order of ear, memory, reflex, synthesis, intelligence, and insights....These children are the ones who are going to become great performers.[3]

---

2. David Henry Feldman with Lynn T. Goldsmith, *Nature's Gambit* (New York: Basic Books, Inc., 1986), p. 4.
3. "Introduction," in Harold C. Schonberg, *The Glorious Ones* (Times Books, New York: Random House, 1985), p. xiii.

By instinct, Marina knew that an exceptional child had to be born with qualities of which Schonberg speaks; by cultural experience, she also knew that environment was indispensable to the development of that special talent. Yo-Yo was born with an inordinate capacity to learn quickly and to perfection. With his phenomenal memory, he absorbed knowledge at an unbelievable pace, retaining all he learned, dazzling all who came in contact with him. Nature had performed one of her wondrous acts in creating a remarkable being. But, like all other children who manifested a mind of their own, he needed motivation and encouragement.

Children thrive on praise; rewards for things well done are an integral part of the learning process. And the learning process requires that the child finds pleasure in the work. No matter what the subject matter, any child, faced with tedium and boredom, rebels. He does not like to work against the grain. Prodigies are no exception.

From the cradle, Yo-Yo was surrounded by a world of music; he heard hundreds of classical selections on records, or played by his father or his sister. Bach and Mozart were engraved in his mind.

From his mother, a former opera singer, he inherited a love for song and always sang in tune. His notes were clear and never sharp or flat.

Wondering how her two-year old child could explain that the pitch was too high or too low, she questioned him. With childish simplicity he would reply "Mommy, I don't know. I just know."

Yo-Yo was unaware of this unique gift, but his mother suspected that her son's talent for music was something special, something to be reckoned with, and when she told her husband, he had to agree.

Destiny had placed a gifted child in their care and it was their responsibility not to let it go to waste. Yo-Yo's talent awed them; finding the right key to channel that talent, that potential to music greatness posed a serious challenge. They thought of their own poverty and their own struggle to survive in the highly competitive field of music. Did they dare direct him on the same road they had travelled?

"Let's just wait and see what life holds, how things develop," Marina suggested. "We'll make music just a part of his education; we'll not try to influence him in any way to become a professional musician."

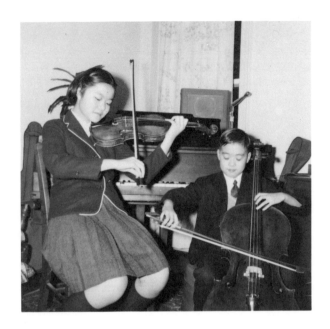

Yo-Yo and Yeou-Cheng. Making music together.

Marina felt that once motivated, a child would go on his own, whether at school, at games with toys, or in any other endeavour.

"You want Yo-Yo to play a string instrument?" she said to her husband. "Very well, let him become interested, and we'll see what happens."

Dr. Ma listened to his wife's rationalization. He listened but remained unconvinced by her words. He had always maintained that it took three generations to produce a good musician. The first generation provided the funds; the second profited from the money by receiving the best education possible, and the third attained the goal set, provided that the right combination of genes was present.

For Hiao-Tsiun Ma, that theory rang true: his father, a wealthy landlord, had provided the necessary funds for him to receive an excellent education. Yo-Yo was the third generation.

But was it fair to impose his dream on his son?

 *5. The Big Instrument*

Marina finished washing the dinner dishes and was sponging off the table. Her husband looked up at her from behind his thick, concave lenses bordered by a silver frame.

"You're right. Our child is very gifted," he began in his calm way. Without mincing words, he announced, "I'm going to make a musician of him."

This sudden revelation did not surprise her, although she wished it would have never come. She knew her husband well, and from past little hints here and there, she suspected that it was just a matter of time when he would do what he always wanted. It couldn't have been otherwise. Still, she made one last attempt.

"Look," she said, "look how hard our lives have been. We both have studied music and pray tell me, where has it got us? We can't even make ends meet."

His face remained impassive.

Appealing to his father's pride, she added, "Do you want our son to suffer the same fate as ours?"

The rhetorical question missed its mark.

For the time being, life went on quietly.

After the crowded condition in their one-room quarters, they considered themselves fortunate to enjoy the luxury of their two-room apartment. Mother and children slept in one room; the other, a smaller bedroom-studio was used by Hiao-Tsiun. Amazingly he had squeezed into that room his piano, a collection of children's string instruments, and his cot. His precious manuscripts and music scores, meticulously arranged by him for children, were jammed into an old armoire and piled up on the piano top. Every corner was bulging with his papers.

Though it was small, Dr. Ma felt comfortable in it. It was his inner sanctum.

In the days that followed, Marina went about her household duties. His decision had left her in a quandary. Was her husband right in persisting? On the other hand, she could not forget the scene that had transpired between Yo-Yo and Yeou-Cheng after her first concert at the University of Paris. Here was a seven-and-a-half-year-old performer asking her little brother, "Well, did you like it? How well did I play?"

Yo-Yo looked at her, his black eyes lighting up. "Sis, dear Sis, you played very well…" He hesitated for a moment, measuring his words. "You were great. But….But you were just a little off tone…"

Marina marvelled at her son's diplomatic way of offering criticism, being careful of his sister's feelings. He was only three years old!

Yeou-Cheng, accepting his observation with curiosity, persisted, "How much off tone was I?" To which he quickly replied in French, "*Une petite virgule*— just a little comma."

The amazing thing about it all was that Yo-Yo was not familiar with a single note of that musical selection!

From that time forth, Yo-Yo would act as Yeou-Cheng's "press agent" every time she performed.

In the lobby he counted people as they arrived and reported back to his sister with great excitement, so much was his delight in her success.

Yo-Yo was alive with life, always ready to say and do something to make others happy. After all, his name meant "friend."

In spite of all the positive signs Yo-Yo was showing, Marina kept making all sorts of excuses for not wanting a musical career for her son. And when Hiao-Tsiun plagued her with "think it over, think of the injustice we may do him if we do not at least try," she would reply, "That's just it; I am thinking of him."

Her heart beat with a different beat from her husband's, yet she was filled with a sense of guilt.

Marina thought it was enough for Yo-Yo to be studying piano, but since Yeou-Cheng had already begun playing a second instrument — a violin — why should she deny the same opportunity to her son? After all, his father could teach him too, using the small-sized violin, which Yeou-Cheng had outgrown and all the music sheets. It would be like a younger child inheriting an older brother's or sister's clothes.

To his father, however, it was evident that Yo-Yo had no real interest in playing the violin, although he was very good at it.

Dr. Ma was perplexed. It was against his pedagogical theory to force a child to make music; he had to do it because he liked it. The problem was resolved when little Yo-Yo said to him, "I don't like the sound violins make; I want a big instrument."

To encourage his gifted son, Dr. Ma said to him, "I'll get one for you, one way or another." But he admonished, "Mind you, once you start with a big instrument, you cannot switch back to the violin. Don't tell me a month from now that you have changed your mind."

Yo-Yo, familiar with the firm tone in his father's voice, knew he meant every word. "I will play it," he stated resolutely. "I won't change my mind."

Patiently, Dr. Ma improvised a "big instrument" by attaching an end pin to a viola. After all, that should satisfy a three-year old. So he thought. But Yo-Yo knew better and proved it at the Conservatory concert he attended with his father.

Yo-Yo sat completely absorbed in what he heard, but especially in what he saw. "I want *that*," he told his father, jumping from his seat as he pointed to a big double-bass on the stage.

"You don't want *that*; it's too big for you. You won't be able to hold it."

Yo-Yo avoided the issue. He knew exactly what he wanted and was bent on getting it.

Struck by the intensity of the request and wanting to make his son happy, especially since he was showing so much self-motivation and determination, Dr. Ma was inclined to go along. Still, he worried lest Yo-Yo might change his mind. He was but a mere child.

He decided to allow a few months to go by, hoping that the matter would be forgotten. But Yo-Yo, persistent, kept reminding him, "When am I going to get the 'big instrument'?"

Partly because of Yo-Yo's insistence, partly because he had faith in his son's promising future, Dr. Ma went to see Monsieur Vatelot, one of

Yo-Yo insisted on playing a "Big Instrument."

Paris's foremost violin makers, for advice.

"Let him have it; I know Yo-Yo. He will give you no peace until he holds a 'big instrument' in his hands." Besides, he added, "I have a feeling it is a sign that something good will come out of it."

They decided upon a cello.

Marina, of course, had been kept in the dark about all these goings-on until her husband brought home the 1/16th cello Monsieur Vatelot had loaned him. That was the last straw for Marina. There was nothing more she could say or do. If that is what my husband wants, all well and good, she thought. Let him pay for the consequences of his actions.

Yo-Yo, of course, was ecstatic and jumped with joy. A 1/16th cello looked very big to a tiny boy.

It was not until much later that Yo-Yo confided to his mother that the real reason he wanted a "big instrument" was to avoid competing with Yeou-Cheng, whom he thought played violin so much better.

Without losing any time, Hiao-Tsiun began giving lessons to his son.

Though exhausted from his own work, each day he sat down patiently with Yo-Yo, exacting the same degree of discipline from him as he, himself, had practiced throughout his life, for discipline went hand in hand with one's growth.

A self-made man, professor of musicology, violinist and composer in his own right, and well-versed in Chinese and French cultures, he tolerated no nonsense. From the very beginning he set forth certain well-defined guidelines for his son's intellectual development. He stressed organization, concentration, memorization, constant practice and, at the head of them all, discipline. Mistakes were acceptable during practice but not at final performances. "Success in life," he held, "does not come easily; a definite goal must be established and all means must be used to attain it."

Memorization continued to play an important part in Yo-Yo's training. Memorization, however, was not meant to be a meaningless exercise. It liberated the musician from dependence on the written score.

Dr. Ma applied the methodology, which he had developed for the teaching of music to children, to his own son, bearing in mind that "music making" was to be a pleasurable experience. Throughout it all, he served as model in carrying out those pedagogical principles to which he himself adhered.

Yo-Yo possessed a formidable and uncanny power of concentration, indispensable to his training. Training alone, however, does not a "boy wonder" make in the world of music. What helped the training along was his insatiable curiosity to learn and achieve — a curiosity that has stayed with him throughout his life.

Yo-Yo feared his father, who believed that fear of the Lord was at the beginning of all knowledge. Marina, sensing the unvoiced resentment and the unexpressed rebellion of her son, often intervened, telling Yo-Yo not to "hate" his father. "It's just his way of handling children," she would explain.

When Dr. Ma was away from home, Yo-Yo took advantage of his absence by occupying his seat at dinner time, flatly stating, "I am daddy, now." The child was then in character, relaxed, laughing, and doing away with all ceremonies and formalities.

Cello lessons continued. Having given Yo-Yo the best of his musical expertise, Dr. Ma knew the time had come to seek out more renowned teachers for further studies. That is what he had done with Yeou-Cheng when he took her to Belgium for violin lessons with the highly respected Arthur Grumiaux. He did the same for Yo-Yo, selecting Mme. Michelle Lepinte, a well-known cello instructor.

Before taking Yo-Yo to Mme. Lepinte, Dr. Ma had used études by Bach for his son's lessons, spending countless hours preparing arrangements and listening patiently while he practiced.

When Mme. Lepinte found out, she frowned upon the choice of composer. "Dr. Ma," she said to him, "why have you chosen Bach for Yo-Yo? He's much too difficult for a child that age."

When Dr. Ma made no reply, she thought it best not to pursue the matter further.

There was no question in Hiao-Tsiun's mind that Yo-Yo could easily accomplish the task by learning only two measures of the music each day. By the second day, he would know four measures. By the third day, he would know six measures, and so on.

When he thought his son ready, he sprang a surprise for Mme. Lepinte, by asking Yo-Yo to play the entire Bach piece. She was dazzled. Never in her long years of teaching had she heard anything like it. The performer was Yo-Yo, but she knew that it was his father's method that had triumphed.

When Yo-Yo was not yet six years old, he was making his début with the same Bach Suite plus a selection from a composition by Paul Bazelaire. Before the concert, however, Yo-Yo told his father that he was going to play "the whole thing," by which he meant the entire eight parts of the composition. His father reminded him that the program listed him as playing one or two selections only. But nothing could dissuade Yo-Yo.

"You can't do that," his father retorted, "if you play the entire suite, it will take much longer than the time they allotted you on the program. The audience will then say, "What kind of parents are we to make a child study so hard? They would not think kindly of us; they would have the impression that we are heartless."

Yo-Yo was quick to understand his father's concern and, of course, would do nothing to cause him pain or embarrassment. He reflected for a few seconds, his mind working at great speed.

"*Bien,*" he said. "O.K. I have an idea." And he went on to outline his strategy.

"When I finish playing the first part," he began, "you applaud. The audience will follow your applause. Then I will play the second part. When I finish, you'll applaud again. And each time I finish another part, you'll applaud again, until the entire eight parts have been played. Each time you applaud, the audience will follow with their applause. In that way, the people can't blame you for letting me play the whole thing, for I would be playing in response to their applause."

He played for almost an hour, and at the end, the audience went wild with applause and shouts of "Bravo!"

"Imagine," Marina recalled, "this was the way Yo-Yo's mind worked — quick as a flash." Then, smiling, she added, "His stubborn streak never left him."

Dr. Ma was well aware that prodigies cannot be created. They can be directed, they can be refined, they can be polished — but the source of genius must be there at birth. Some are discovered; others are "born to blush unseen," as a poet once wrote. Part of Yo-Yo's training may have advanced through discipline, but deep in his heart, Yo-Yo loved music and strove to achieve beyond his years, beyond the instruction he received. He practiced his music dutifully and when praised for the "work-out," he was as happy as any other child who received a pat on the head.

Marina remained still unconvinced that the road her husband had chosen for Yo-Yo was the right one. Dr. Ma, on the other hand, never wavered in his conviction that he was dealing with a budding virtuoso. He owed it to himself to do all in his power to guide his son toward the goal he had set. He knew that a truly precocious child with a high I. Q. should be brought up outside expected conventions; he knew that training should start while the child was still young and yielding to authority. He also knew that the task he had set for himself would not be an easy one. The road would have many twists and turns, but at the end of the journey Yo-Yo would be worlds away from most of his peers. He had chosen a solitary road for his son, but he was confident that ultimately Yo-Yo would climb to an enviable height, soaring among the stars.

After all, Marina's and his own background more than qualified them for the task.

And that would make all the difference.

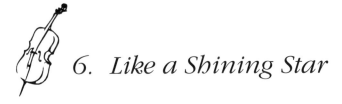

6. Like a Shining Star

T hough strongly opposed to a career in music for Yo-Yo, Marina was nevertheless happy that he was studying it. She felt music enriched the life of children as well as that of adults. Like poetry and painting, music elevated the spirit.

One day, she heard Yo-Yo playing in the studio. What she heard astonished her. Quietly and unobserved she entered the room. Her eyes fell immediately on his long, slender fingers. She could not believe the music they were drawing out of that instrument. She riveted her eyes on the position of his hands: he had already understood exact phrasing. The bow itself was breathing life into the music. That kind of phrasing haunted her; it resembled closely the way a singer projects her voice during a performance. Incredibly, Yo-Yo had reached that height in just a few lessons, an extraordinary feat for a child just over three years old.

That evening, Marina could hardly wait for her husband to return home. She barely contained her emotions. "I have a confession to make," she blurted out, hardly giving him a chance to remove his jacket. "And I know what you're going to say. But I must admit that you were right." Her eyes brightened. "Our son should have a career in music. I listened to his playing today and I am thoroughly convinced: his bow has a voice."

"I'm glad to hear you say what I have known all along." He paused for a moment, relieved to learn that the differences they had had about their son's career could at last be put away.

"I knew you'd come around to my way of thinking," he said, half in jest, half in earnest. He could not mask his elation at being vindicated. "Yes, Yo-Yo does play like a shining star," he had to admit.

Totally immersed in his music.

There were already good qualities about his playing: the way he held the bow, the adroit fingering, the technique he had so readily acquired. With his formidable memory, Yo-Yo had no difficulty in learning and retaining anything he studied. His power of concentration was phenomenal, so totally immersed was he in his music.

Marina noted that whenever she walked into the room during his practice sessions, he did not react like other children, who were normally distracted from what they were doing. Not Yo-Yo. He remained oblivious to everything but his cello playing until he had finished his lesson. Then he became a completely changed boy; he would jump up and start leaping like a frog around the room.

That special gift Yo-Yo had with the bow was well understood by his mother, who had been trained to become an opera singer. But the meaning was beyond Yo-Yo's grasp when she told him that he made his bow "sing" when he played.

"What do you mean, Mommy?" he asked in his childish way.

"Well....Someday I'll explain it to you. But not now. Someday, when you're older."

Making those strings sing out what he felt within him.

The Mas in Paris.

Was it Destiny or was it his father's will that Yo-Yo became a cello virtuoso? No one will ever know. Certainly it did not just happen. His parents' cultural background was bound to rub off on him. And that too, made a difference.

The language Yo-Yo first heard and learned from his parents was Chinese. In Paris, however, he was exposed to another language. This cultural duality made him aware of his own ethnic background, which stressed obedience, hard-work, endurance, patience and discipline. As he grew older, he could never forget his bi-cultural upbringing, which played such a major role in the development of his personality.

Marina never used baby talk with her son. Wise in her mother's ways, she never put a damper on his childish curiosity. When he asked a question — and he asked many — she elaborated her answers as if she were conversing with an adult. No inquiry was insignificant or foolish, she told him, if it stimulated intellectual growth. She encouraged good thinking, rewarding him with a "Bravo, Yo-Yo, that was a good question."

Bedtime was a moment of intimate sharing. The room Marina occupied with her two children had bunk beds. Yeou-Cheng slept on the upper bed, while Marina took the lower one, with Yo-Yo's cot close to her. There were no bedtime stories. Instead, she asked her children, "What did you do today?" According to their answers, she would advise and guide them relying on ancient Chinese tenets of behaviour. She stressed the importance of kindness, generosity and selflessness, placing a high value on the forgiveness of those who may have hurt their feelings. "Always strive to have a positive outlook on life," she reiterated.

And as their heavy lids slowly closed and the words "Always strive to have a positive outlook on life," sank into the subconscious of their minds, they fell asleep.

But sleep did not come easily to Marina. She lay awake, staring at the darkness in the room, searching in the pool of her memories.

Now she could think back calmly on those earlier days of her life that, at that time, seemed to be a nightmare from which there was no awakening....

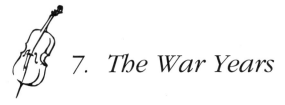

7. *The War Years*

I n the Orient, a father's wish was tantamount to a command; that's the way children were raised from the beginning. Marina fully realized this when her father had to make a major decision in the face of political events.

Marina Ma, née Ya-Wen Lo, the youngest of six children — two boys and four girls — was born in Hong Kong in 1923. Like so many other middle-class Chinese, her father, a rice and seafood merchant, believed that only through education could one succeed in life. He taught his children that it was the surest way to gain honour and prestige for themselves and for the entire family.

While life was peaceful and uneventful in the Lo family, dark clouds of war were gathering about. Fortunately, Hong Kong felt secure under British protection with its powerful naval base in Shanghai. Walking a tight rope, Hong Kong skillfully managed not to become embroiled in mainland China's internecine battles for power.

All this political intrigue did not trouble Ya-Wen, concerned as she was with her studies. But not for long. Events were soon to change her attitude.

When the entire world finally became engulfed in war, fear shook Hong Kong to its very foundation. Begun in the West, the Second World War had spread to the Far East. With Japan's attack on the U.S. naval base at Pearl Harbour on 7 December 1941, a second major front was opened in the Pacific. Having secured their northern flank in China by the signing of a treaty with Russia, the Japanese began moving southward.

The British, assailed in Europe, had neither the heart nor the resources to carry out their responsibilities in Asia and withdrew from

Shanghai and north China ports in August. They retained, however, their naval base at Singapore and held onto Hong Kong.

Perceiving weakness in the British position, the Japanese saw an opportunity for their navy to attack. Japan's dire need of new sources of materials led to a relentless drive for the conquest of surrounding lands. Hong Kong was strategically positioned. The Japanese moved with lightning speed, as their pilots rained tons of bombs on the once peaceful, commercial centre. Eighteen days after Pearl Harbour, on 25 December, Hong Kong capitulated.

Thousands of people had been killed. The wounded were so numerous it was useless attempting to get a count.

Emboldened by so many military victories, Japan continued to occupy more and more territories, pursuing a policy that would make her the dominant power in the East. It was this ambitious policy that led to her demise, for it forced the different Chinese political factions to unite as never before against a common enemy.

Attacks in the early forties had forced a large number of people to migrate from Chungking to west China. The educational system, so prized by the Chinese, was disrupted, and students and faculties of most Eastern colleges fled via an overland truck route to makeshift quarters.

Anticipating a dearth of food supplies, people began a systematic hoarding of goods. Political corruption ran rampant.

Resistance to the invasion, which had been sporadic and factional, was now carried along a united front as the Communists, using guerrilla tactics, began to collaborate with the Central government.

As the Communist factions became more and more numerous, however, they began fighting one another for political control of territories, each faction forging ahead for its own advantage. The unity that had been gained against Japan, their common enemy, disintegrated and the danger of renewed civil war loomed on the horizon.

By the year 1944, the Chinese had suffered excessive losses. The Japanese were now spearheading their drive toward Chungking.

Inflation reached an alarming level and profiteers exploited all angles to reap huge profits. A great number of the population, including government employees and teachers, failed to receive salaries.

Conditions were ripe for the Communists to score great successes among the peasants who lived behind the Japanese lines.

With the end of the war and the surrender of Japan to the Allies on 2 September 1945, political unification in China was an illusion. The Communists were in reality the victors. Social revolution ensued.

No revolutionary spirit, however, not even the tyranny of war, which forebode a new, dark world, was sufficient to sway Ya-Wen's father from his determination to find a way for his daughter to complete her education. She had only one year to finish high school — still it would have been folly for her to remain in Hong Kong.

During his waking hours, he racked his brain to find a way out of his dilemma. Even while lying in bed at night, unable to sleep, he pondered the problem. Then, as if in a dream, he had the solution: Why not send her to a boarding school on the mainland, where she would be safe?

Ya-Wen remained silent when her father made his decision known. Only her eyes betrayed the hurt and the sadness she felt inside. But he had spoken and she had to abide by his will.

"I can see that you are hurt and that you are holding back your tears. But I know the wound will eventually heal. We shall all be sad; however, it is your future I'm thinking about." He spoke in a solemn tone. Then added, "My child, your mind is like a blossom which must open to become a pretty flower."

She understood. The separation would break his heart as much as hers. She knew that.

The long and difficult journey to Canton did not require a great deal of preparation. She was to travel with two other girls, family neighbours, also going away to continue with their studies.

It was the first time Ya-Wen was away from home. She missed her family terribly. Not once, however, did she allow her homesickness to interfere with her studies. Her spirit was buoyed by the thought that the year would soon be over and, after graduating from high school, she would be back with her loved ones.

A letter from her father, however, quickly shattered her hopes.

"My dearest daughter," he began, "I know how much you have looked forward to coming home; surely you know how much we've missed you. But I must tell you that conditions here, in Hong Kong, have reached a highly dangerous point, and I fear for the safety of us all.

"Your sister, who's gone to live in the southern part of the mainland, agrees with me that it would be best for you to join her there, where you'll be safe."

Safe in southern China? He was wrong. The Japanese had already invaded the area.

That summer, the worsening news from home and the pressures from tests for admission to Central University in Chungking took their toll on the school girl. But she had resolved to succeed at all costs. Although mentally and emotionally drained, at the end she was admitted to the university.

Meanwhile, fate was weaving an unexpected twist in the web of her life.

8. *Ya-Wen Meets Hiao-Tsiun*

Student life at Central University could not have been more pleasurable for Ya-Wen. She was studying the subject she loved best: music, concentrating mainly on voice and opera courses. Her goal was to become a lyric soprano.

Originally, the University Centre had been located in Nanking, but the Japanese occupation had forced the entire complex to move to Chungking — a Herculean task but the only safe way to insure the continuity of higher learning.

Ya-Wen did not realize at the time that her father had been wise in sending her to school away from home. Later, as a mother, she would fully appreciate his love for her and the sacrifices he had made. Right now all she felt was the stinging pain of separation from her loved ones.

Life, however, had its compensations. Out of suffering came a great joy.

At Central University, Ya-Wen laid eyes on Hiao-Tsiun Ma, her professor of music theory. He was tall, lean and handsome, with jet black hair framing his face. Her heart was pierced by his intense look, as he stood before the class, a striking picture of dignity and scholarship. As she took notes on his lecture, she experienced a strange, weakening sensation, which she had never before felt in the presence of any other man.

Ya-Wen learned that one of her schoolmates with whom she had become friendly was Dr. Ma's sister. Hesitant at first to reveal her interest in her professor, she eventually gathered the courage to ask, "Tsiun-Cheng, tell me about your brother."

Tsiun-Cheng was not entirely unaware of Ya-Wen's veiled interest in her brother as a man. "There's not very much to tell," she began, "he's a very private person. He was born in Ningbo (on 11 July 1911), just south of Shanghai. Having become disenchanted with the political conditions in China, he went to Paris to further his musical career. That was back in 1936. He adapted himself to the new bi-cultural life and was very happy. When Central University offered him a teaching position, he returned to China, where you see him now."

Ya-Wen stood there, drinking in every word in silence. A thousand convoluted thoughts raced through her mind. Her expression, however, was an open book. Tsiun-Cheng guessed what she really wanted to know and did not dare ask outright.

"No, he doesn't have a fiancée." Then she added, "Do you really like him that much?"

Ya-Wen, embarrassed, nodded girlishly. She wasn't ready to disclose it to her friend, fearing ridicule. Still, without taking her mind off music, her heart began singing a different tune.

Marina Ma, Shanghai, 1947.

Meanwhile, the Japanese were advancing rapidly, forcing the Chinese Resistance to retreat farther and farther to the inner mainland.

In the midst of the upheaval, with the impending danger threatening them, students at the University had no heart to apply themselves seriously to intellectual pursuits. Mentally stressed out, they did not measure up to Dr. Ma's exacting standards. He could well understand, empathize and sympathize with them, but what he could not tolerate was their indifference toward their school work. For him, a perfectionist, there was no excuse for not fulfilling one's responsibilities. Instead of allowing his students to wallow in pessimism, he exhorted them to redouble their efforts in the face of adversity. He was a captain who did not retreat even when the odds were overwhelming. His exhortations, nevertheless, fell on deaf ears.

Disillusioned with the performance of his students, he left his teaching position and returned to Paris in order to devote himself completely to music theory and composition.

The Japanese continued to press on relentlessly with the occupation of mainland China. The more fortunate people escaped still farther inland; others had no choice but to resign themselves to their fate.

Ya-Wen kept abreast of events in Hong Kong, and the news she received from home added to her determination to go back. She thought she was very selfish to remain at a safe distance from danger, while her own family was caught in the fray. She thought and thought, but with each thought she arrived at the same conclusion. Returning to Hong Kong was the only thing to do. It was the right thing. She was confident that somehow she would find a way to continue with her studies.

She shared her decision with Tsiun-Cheng, in whom by this time, she confided.

"I've decided to go back home. It's best that I do. Yet I must not hold back something from you — for the longest time I've dreamed of going to Paris."

Ya-Wen felt good about voicing her pent-up emotions.

"I've heard so much about that enlightened city. I'm so eager to see it."

"Of course," her friend replied, tongue-in-cheek. And maybe you'll get a chance to see my brother again."

The two smiled at each other.

This time, it was Tsiun-Cheng's turn to take Ya-Wen into her confidence. "I've had the same idea. Maybe we could go to Paris together."

"I never thought of that. And why not? It sounds great." The two girls made a pact.

Having said that, Ya-Wen reflected further. "But first I must return to Hong Kong to be with my family and earn enough money for all the expenses needed."

And so she did.

Having accomplished her purpose, Ya-Wen and her friend set off for Paris. Tsiun-Cheng lost no time in introducing Ya-Wen to her brother.

Marina was greatly impressed by Hiao-Tsiun's politeness and gentlemanly bearing; she did not fail to miss the twinkle in his eyes as he spoke to her. But in the classroom, although she was awed by the depth of knowledge he imparted to his students, she was disturbed by the strict discipline he demanded of them. To her, he seemed unduly stern. It was a trait which gave her strong misgivings: Was it just his technique of teaching or was it an inherent quality of his character? Would he also be severe as her husband, she wondered. She soon dismissed these thoughts preferring to dwell upon his finer qualities, which overshadowed this trait. Realizing how much their backgrounds were alike and how music would fill their souls with happiness, she submerged her doubts.

On 17 July 1949, they were married and Ya-Wen became Mrs. Hiao-Tsiun Ma. The young bride was happy; not only could she continue with her music, she had now another meaningful purpose to her life.

After mastering the technique of singing, she enrolled at the École Française. What she needed now was further training in the projection of her voice, which she accomplished after countless hours of practice. Then she enrolled at the renowned École César Franck, from which she was graduated.

Bride and groom on their Wedding Day.

The time had come, however, for her to make an important choice: Embark on an opera career or devote herself to the raising of a family. It was a major decision and one that demanded a great deal of sacrifice. She chose family over career.

Their first child, a girl, was called Marie-Thérèse, but in keeping with Chinese tradition, they also named her Yeou-Cheng, which means, "May you have lots of friends."

Four years later, when Yo-Yo, also known as Ernest, was born, Dr. Ma was still earning a meagre salary. Still, he was able to make ends meet, thanks to the additional money he received from his brother, who had migrated to Chicago. One way or another, he managed to have his children study music. As for Marina, the education of her children had priority over all else.

They had survived the war years in the Orient; they had coped with the cold and the poverty in the new land.

Now, as Marina lay in bed, sharing her room with her two children, she wondered whether it was through fatigue or self-pity or her reminiscences of the past that brought calmness to her. She heard Yeou-Cheng moving in the bunk above her and took one last look at Yo-Yo's cot. Night was sweet as sleep fell upon her. She knew that with the dawn, her spirit would be renewed.

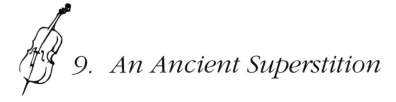

9. An Ancient Superstition

Yo-Yo shouted, "I don't want you to die, Mommy. I don't want you to die!"

Marina was taken aback by this unexpected outcry from Yo-Yo. The words had a freezing effect on her.

"What are you saying, Yo-Yo? What kind of nonsense is this? Who told you I was going to die?"

Yo-Yo looked at his mother wide-eyed, fear written on his face. Impulsively, Marina put a hand around his neck and drew him close to her.

"Now, tell me, who put that silly idea into your head? I'm not going to die."

Yo-Yo freed himself from his mother's tight hold and drew a deep breath. "Look. See?" And he indicated a point of hair growing down the middle of his forehead. "Mr. Choo said that it's a curse put there and that one of my parents would surely die."

Marina bit her lip. That old superstition was still being kept alive, she thought. Nothing but a stupid superstition! She knew it was just a form of folklore, a legend veiled in obscurity, which old-time Chinese insisted on perpetuating as part of their cultural heritage. Too well-educated to place any stock on such absurdity, Marina dismissed any thought of superstition connected to that growth of black hair on her son's forehead. Rather than presaging misfortune, for her it was simply an ugly sight. Eventually, it had to be removed despite the pain it would cause him. As yet, however, she had not found the courage to go through with it.

"Who put the 'curse' on me, Mommy?" Yo-Yo insisted.

Evidently, Mr. Choo's words had made an indelible impression on the young child's mind.

"Yo-Yo, Yo-Yo, *mon pauvre petit* — my poor, little boy, there's no curse on you. Mr. Choo is just a silly old neighbour; he shouldn't go around saying things like that. Don't pay any attention to him."

Yo-Yo would not listen. He thought she was lying to spare his feelings.

"Please, Mommy, please, cut it off, cut it off!"

Marina tried to discourage him, but Yo-Yo remained adamant. From past experience, she knew he was going to have his way.

"Very well, Yo-Yo. I'll do it not because of a silly superstition, mind you, but because it will make your forehead smoother and more handsome." She hesitated for a moment.

"I want you to know, however, that the hair cannot be cut off. It has to be plucked, one strand at a time. It's the only way for it not to grow back. It will hurt. It will hurt a lot."

"I don't care. I want you to do it. I don't want you to die."

Patiently, carefully, Marina pulled out each hair, cringing as she kept repeating, "Am I hurting you? Do you want me to stop?"

Yo-Yo tightened the muscles around his eyes and clenched his small fists to resist the pain.

"No, Mommy, it doesn't hurt. It doesn't hurt," he bleated.

Not until his mother had completed the job and dusted talcum powder on his forehead did Yo-Yo start bawling. He ran to Yeou-Cheng, his *petite mère* — little mother — as Marina referred to her, seeking comfort.

With the removal of that point of hair from her son's forehead, Marina hoped that she had put an end to any superstitious notions that Yo-Yo might hear from Mr. Choo or his ilk.

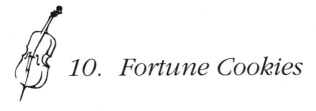

10. Fortune Cookies

At 10:30 in the morning, on a Tuesday, the doorbell rang. Marina remembered the time and the day because she was expecting a visit from one of her friends. When she opened the door, however, she saw the postman.

"*Bonjour Mme Ma*," he greeted her in his usual friendly manner, "there's a package for you. It's from America."

Marina thanked him and carried the package into the kitchen. When she glanced at the sender's return address, she exclaimed, "Oh, *mon Dieu*! It's from my sister in California; I thought she had forgotten me." Her eyes shifted to the cancelled stamps. One of them portrayed the Statue of Liberty, with her right hand raised high, holding a torch. For a moment she recalled a small model of the statue on the far end of the *Île de la Cité*, the islet where the magnificent cathedral of Notre Dame stands. Not until she saw that stamp, however, did that symbol reveal its true meaning to her: "Liberty!" She cut off the stamp and saved it in a drawer along with other mementos.

The package contained a collection of sundry items hard to come by in postwar Paris. What intrigued Marina most of all was a small plastic bag containing odd-shaped cookies. "These are fortune cookies," her sister had written. "I don't think you've seen them before, but here, in America, they are very popular. Enjoy them with your children."

Marina tore open the plastic and began transferring the contents into a ceramic jar, intending to ration them out to her children. In the process, a cookie fell onto the table. How original, she thought, cookies with a message. Filled with curiosity, she cracked open the cookie, pulled out the narrow paper ribbon and slowly began to decipher the cryptic message: "You will soon embark on a long voyage."

Marina laughed to herself, "Wouldn't that be wonderful? Those Americans! They can think up all sorts of things." And then she went about finishing what she had started. But the strange message came back repeatedly like a haunting tune of a song or a verse from a poem long forgotten.

Not a month had gone by when a letter arrived. "It's from your brother," Marina said. Hiao-Tsiun opened it immediately. He was always happy to get news from him. Avidly he read every word but his eyes focused on one line at the end of the letter. He read it a second time to be sure he had understood correctly: *"...And so I have decided to go back to China with my wife and child."*

(From left to right) Dr. Ma's brother, Hiao-Jone Ma, Marina,
Dr. Hiao-Tsiun Ma, Yo-Yo (age $5\frac{1}{2}$) and Yeou-Cheng (age 10)
(Chicago, 1961).

Hiao-Tsiun's face became ashen white. "My brother must be out of his mind," he told Marina, "he wants to go back to China. Has he forgotten the chaos in that country? How does he expect to make a living when there are no jobs? I must take those crazy thoughts out of his mind."

Without wasting time, he sat down to write his brother, entreating him to abandon his plans. *"You don't make sense,"* he told him. *"Going back to China at this time is pure folly. Don't you keep up with what's going on there?"*

To make sure his brother got the message, he followed up with a long distance call. But to no avail.

"My brother refuses to listen to me," Hiao-Tsiun told his wife. "He's making a big mistake and I'm very worried."

Marina looked at her husband. She had lived with him long enough to read his mind even before he informed her of the decision he had made. His expressive face mirrored every emotion, which he controlled with just enough restraint.

"I already know what you're going to tell me," she said. "Do what you must. Your brother has always helped us out. Now it's our turn."

"We must leave for the United States as soon as possible. Maybe I can talk some sense into him if I see him in person."

The message in the fortune cookie! Marina recalled. Had she been superstitious she might have been troubled by the content and the timing of that message.

The Mas took all their emergency savings, sold whatever valuables they had, and booked passage to New York. Since Yo-Yo was under age, they did not have to pay for his ticket. For that extra savings, they were very grateful.

After landing in New York, the family went directly to the brother's house in Rochester, where they remained for a month.

Using all his persuasive skills, Hiao-Tsiun succeeded in dissuading his brother from going to China and in convincing him that it was to his advantage to complete his doctoral degree. Eventually, when conditions in China became stabilized, there would be no reason for him not to go there.

It was in Rochester that a new door opened for the five-and-a-half-year-old prodigy. There, Yo-Yo gave his first American concert at Nazareth College.

It was a tense moment for Marina as she watched her son carrying his instrument to the stage. Sitting beside her husband, she followed the music with suspended breath. She knew each note by heart. Her eyes never left the stage as Yo-Yo performed like a professional. She looked closely at the serious expression on his face mirroring the intensity of his feelings for the composition he was interpreting, and she marvelled at the dexterity of his fingering up and down the unfretted fingerboard. For some unexplained reason, her eyes shifted to the audience and she wondered what was going on in their minds as they listened, enraptured by the music. Could they ever believe by any stretch of the imagination that that very little boy, whom they perceived totally wrapped up in his music, could be the same little mischievous rascal she knew him to be?

For a fleeting moment she allowed her thoughts to wander back to their apartment in Paris, her mind sifting through episodes dear to her heart. She was thankful that despite the strict upbringing and the emotional strain to which Yo-Yo had been subjected as a child, he had managed to retain a great sense of humour. He was a survivor, who had preserved that extra human dimension that set him apart from ordinary children, that extra "something light" that endeared him to everyone. Her mind unlocked a stream of thoughts like the ebb and flow of a tide that reluctantly reaches the shore only to retreat back into the open sea, leaving irregular patterns on the wet sand.

Involuntarily, an old Chinese saying crept across her mind: "Poor quality iron does not make good nails, and good men do not make good soldiers." During the Sino-Japanese War, however, the old saying was cleverly twisted to: "Good men make good soldiers," as a morale booster for the fighting men.

The adage had made a deep impression on Dr. Ma, and when he heard his two-year old son singing a song about frogs, he called Marina aside and told her, "Our son is a little good for nothing. He's like the "iron" in the Chinese adage; he doesn't have the right stuff to turn him into a "good thing."

Of course Marina was surprised to hear her husband talk so negatively about their son; he had always praised Yo-Yo for his intelligence and predicted that someday he would be somebody.

"What makes you say that?" she remembered asking.

"Well," he answered, "you know the song Yo-Yo keeps singing while he goes about leaping like a frog? The one that goes:

I'm a frog
Always in the field
Jumping up and down
And I sing: Co-co-co-co-co.

Marina remembered that song very well, and she nodded.

"He doesn't realize," her husband continued, "that he should stop singing when he comes to: 'Co-co-co-co-co'; instead he keeps repeating the last line as if he forgets when the song ends. Yo-Yo has such a poor memory," he said, punctuating his last words and shaking his head in disbelief.

And that was when Marina chuckled. "How do you expect the poor child to know? He's only two years old!"

As it turned out, it did not take Yo-Yo too long to prove that he was not made of "poor quality iron" and that his wit and resourcefulness were sharper than the best of nails, as his father soon learned.

Knowing his son to be quite mischievous, Dr. Ma warned him never to disturb his sister while she was playing piano. "I forbid you to go into the studio while Yeou-Cheng practices," he had admonished.

Although Yo-Yo knew there would be the devil to pay if he disobeyed his father, little rascal that he was, he took his father's words literally. Instead of going into the room, he stood at the threshold. From there he took perfect aim at his sister and pelted her with spit balls. He trusted Yeou-Cheng not to breathe a word to their father and he had his little fun. It was his moment of triumph for, in his conscience, he had succeeded in outwitting his father.

Marina could never get over the quickness of her son's mind and how he could get out of difficulties at the drop of a hat with such a disarming air of innocence.

Her stream of conscience continued to flow like a soothing,

healing balm. In her mind she saw Yeou-Cheng playing piano, using the foot pedals, and Yo-Yo sneaking in and crawling under the piano stool. He then held down the pedals so that his sister could no longer operate them.

In the next room, Dr. Ma was busy writing orchestral arrangements, his ears tuned in on the notes Yeou-Cheng was playing. Suddenly, he put the music sheets aside and listened intently. Something was wrong. He rushed into the room and caught Yo-Yo in the act.

For a moment the room became very small while Dr. Ma loomed above Yo-Yo like an angry giant, his eyes severe and motionless.

Caught totally by surprise, Yo-Yo looked up from his crouched position. When he saw the red in his father's eyes, he quickly composed himself, assuming the pained aspect of someone in distress.

"What are you doing under there?" Dr. Ma bellowed.

"Ah, Papa," Yo-Yo began, regulating his breathing — the saliva having gone dry in his mouth — his face showing the grieved perplexity of a child wondering what really terrible offense he was committing, "I must have dropped my *colophane*— my rosin — when I was playing my cello in this room this morning. I've been looking for it everywhere....I thought it might have rolled under the piano pedals..."

He felt a slight sense of guilt for deceiving his father, but this was not the time to worry over that; it was the time for self-preservation.

What could his poor father do? He knew his son was lying but at the same time he marvelled at Yo-Yo's quick thinking. There was merit in that. It was not like him to go back to his work without first dealing with Yo-Yo's disobedience. He was still angry but at the same time pleased that his mettled son had managed to outwit him once again.

When Yo-Yo was five years old, he gave a piano and cello recital at the University of Paris, in the same hall where Yeou-Cheng had previously performed. He was a tremendous success, playing with great control and authority. Among those in the same Paris Conservatory who greatly admired and respected Yo-Yo was a certain professor, who, in spite of the great age difference between the two, had become a close friend.

One day, both he and Yo-Yo played in a concert under the musical direction of Dr. Ma. At one point, Yo-Yo made a mistake, which he was reluctant to admit. Later, when the professor and he were alone, they discussed the merits of the concert.

"*Monsieur le Professeur*," Yo-Yo began with a straight face, "I'm truly sorry about what happened during the concert. But, don't worry, the mistake you made was hardly noticeable." Then with an air of a seasoned critic he added, "After all, we're all allowed to make mistakes now and then."

The professor, who had the greatest respect for Yo-Yo's professionalism and looked upon him as a budding prodigy, was mortified. Visibly embarrassed by what Yo-Yo was telling him, he went so far as to apologize, convinced that it was he indeed who had played the false note.

A burst of applause shook Marina out of her reverie. Bow in one hand, cello in the other, Yo-Yo was standing, serenely acknowledging the applause with repeated bows like a true pro.

Marina glanced at her husband, who had joined the audience in the thunderous applause, then shifted her eyes back to the stage. A smile across her lips underscored the pride she felt — the pride of a mother remembering the little boy who used to go around leaping like a frog after he had finished playing a piece.

Following this performance, the family travelled to Berkeley, California, for a brief visit with Marina's sister. When the two were alone, Marina confided, "Do you remember those cookies you sent me? Well, my 'fortune' did come true. Coming to the United states was 'a long voyage,'" she added with an impish twinkle in her eyes.

Of course, her sister didn't quite understand what Marina was talking about, but she nodded her head in agreement seeing Marina so happy.

11. An Unexpected Contract

S aying "good-bye" to loved ones is never pleasant; it leaves a void as if a piece of the heart is being torn away. Being with her sister, talking over the things they had done together as children, remembering the quietness of the seashore they could see from their home in Hong Kong and the closeness of family renewed Marina's spirit. But the clock had counted the hours and the calendar had numbered the days. One last embrace, one more renewed promise to write to each other more often, and one more expressed good wish for the future. Another "good-bye" at the airport, and the Mas boarded the plane bound for New York for their eventual return trip to France.

During the time that they stayed in Manhattan, Dr. Ma managed to cover half the city on foot. He liked what he saw: yellow cabs scurrying to and fro; the luxurious window displays along 5th Avenue; Central Park with its children's playgrounds and wide, open spaces. There, people could enjoy strolling or finding a quiet place to read or chat. The ethnic flavour of 2nd Avenue made a marked impression on him, so did the bustle of crowded Chinatown. He was dazzled by the Great White Way with all its bright lights. Those lights helped him to see the future with new courage and new hope. What caused him even more emotional excitement than the brightness of Broadway was a building on West 57th Street. There, he stood silent in front of the imposing façade of Carnegie Hall, the Mecca of all performing artists who aspired to achieve their crowning glory. He stood there in reverent awe as if before a temple of worship and dreamed that one day, with careful planning and drive, he would see his son's name in big, bold letters. A surge of hope filled his heart.

When he went home, that evening, he told Marina, "Before we go back to Paris, I think our children should give a recital here."

Marina stood there dumbfounded. She was used to her husband's sudden announcements, but this time she thought he must be really out of his mind.

Hiao-Tsiun told Marina what he planned to do. Per usual, she listened patiently, not wishing to dampen his enthusiasm. At the same time she thought her husband was acting far too hastily, on mere impulse. To counter him and make him see the reality of things,

Carnegie Hall
(Courtesy of the Carnegie Hall Corporation.)

she gently reminded him, "You and your dreams! And where will you get the money to rent a place?"

Half in jest, half in earnest, he answered, "I was really hoping to get a room in Carnegie Hall…"

She didn't allow him to finish the sentence.

"This time you must really have your head in the clouds."

He completely ignored her remark and continued as if she had never interrupted him.

"…But, of course, I know that we don't have the money. One of my brother's friends suggested that I contact the pastor of a Catholic church nearby where they would make their auditorium available free of charge."

Marina breathed a sigh of relief.

Was Dr. Ma in fact acting on impulse? Perhaps. But he did not have the luxury of time working for him. New York offered a challenge, an opportunity which he dared not miss. God knows when he would be back in the United States, if ever. Was it folly even to think that he could make things happen? Of course not, he was forever the optimist.

Yo-Yo and Yeou-Cheng gave a brilliant joint recital, which was shortly followed by another recital at the Chinese-American Society on Riverside Drive. The unexpected outcome was an invitation to Dr. Ma to be Director of Music and help establish a Children's Orchestra at the Trent School — a small independent primary school in Manhattan — whose representative had been in the audience.

A children's orchestra! Why, he had always dreamed of one. Instantly, a billboard announcing a future recital by Yo-Yo at Carnegie Hall quickly flashed across his mind. New York was the centre of performing arts. It was an illusion; still, he promised himself to work the rest of his life to turn that illusion into reality.

Marina could hardly believe the good fortune that had come their way when her husband told her about the offer at the Trent School. It was a miracle for which she had not prayed. For the time being, there was little else to do but to go back to Paris, put their affairs in order and prepare for their eventual return to the United States. At long last a stream of light was banishing the gloomy shadows of their past.

12. Ormesson

Spring was just ending and the school year at Trent School would not begin until September, but Dr. Ma started packing his treasured music sheets with the arrangements he had made for a children's orchestra. He assembled the string instruments scattered in that two-room apartment and procured others. Monsieur Vatelot, the *lutier*, proved to be more than generous in letting him have additional instruments on credit and insuring that they were all in good condition. Friends were calling or stopping by to express their best wishes and bid them well in their venture in the United States. All was proceeding according to plans. Still, he pondered over and over his decision. Was he doing the best thing for his family? Was it really to their advantage to leave France for a new land? He loved Paris but the idea of settling down in New York appealed even more to him. What he had seen of the city's youth and vigour excited him. All things considered, he concluded that making his permanent home there was the right thing to do.

Though his mind was assailed by opposing thoughts, Hiao-Tsiun never allowed himself to be distracted from his work, nor did he permit his children to be remiss in their tasks. Yo-Yo and Yeou-Cheng continued with their school work and their music. Supplementary lessons in Chinese given by their father were part of their daily assignments. Language and culture continued to receive attention as part of their God-given heritage.

One Sunday morning, shortly after 11:00, there was a knock at their door. Marina went to open it and as soon as she saw the visitor, she called out to her husband, "Look who's here to see you? It's our old friend, Mr. Tso."

The Mas had known him from the time of their wedding. Like Hiao-Tsiun, Mr. Tso was born in Ningbo and had settled in Paris, where he managed his own real estate agency.

Though he told them he had come to congratulate Dr. Ma and express his hope that the family would be happy in America, he withheld from them the other reason for his coming. After getting through with the usual amenities, Mr. Tso asked them if they would like to go for a drive with him to a little suburban town, not too far from Paris. "It would do the whole family good," he said. "After which, we'll go to eat in a little restaurant I know. It's sort of a celebration among friends."

Yo-Yo and Yeou-Cheng were excited. It wasn't often they went car riding. Besides, it was Sunday and they had already finished practicing their music.

It took but a half hour to reach Ormesson from the centre of Paris.

Sister and brother in the Ormesson Garden (1962).

Surprisingly, instead of going to a restaurant Mr. Tso stopped the car in front of a modest house.

"I'd like for you to look at this house," he said. "It doesn't seem like much right now, but the owners are very eager to sell. What they're asking is well below its value."

When he saw the astonished look on the Mas' faces, he hastened to add, "I know; it will need a lot of repairs, but most of it is cosmetic. It will not require a lot of money. Besides, now that you'll be teaching in America, you'll be able to make regular payments on the mortgage."

Hiao-Tsiun grinned, "It is an interesting house, but you must be joking."

Mr. Tso wasn't listening and went on to describe how the work could be done by subcontractors — he knew several who would take on the job — and even offered to supervise the renovations for free.

A thousand thoughts were racing through Hiao-Tsiun's mind. He was intrigued by the idea of having a *pied-à-terre* when the family returned to France during summer vacation. The apartment in Paris would no longer be suitable.

As if the friend had read his mind, he added, "You don't have to decide on the spot. Let's go inside, look around, and then we'll talk. Just remember that these opportunities don't come very often…and you'll have a summer place in France. Think it over…"

Dr. Ma was indeed thinking it over and so was his wife.

Marina envisioned the garden she would plant in the area in front of the house — it was a good, sunny spot. Bright, lovely flowers would adorn either side of the path leading to the front of the door. And, oh to breathe fresh air for a change! Her enthusiasm knew no bounds when she beheld several fruit-bearing trees. Her greatest desire, however, was to feel part of a neighbourhood, where everyone knew and greeted one another — an impossible situation in a big apartment building. Owning one's own piece of land made for stability.

Once before she had savoured vicariously the joy of living in a private home. That was a few years back when Madame Hauch-Corne, a friend of Dr. Ma's, had offered them her beach house in Bretagne. Fully aware of their financial situation, she said, "The house is at your

Husband and wife in their Ormesson Garden.

disposal during the summer months. My administrative responsibilities at the museum will not allow me to take the time off." Then she added delicately, "Outside of paying for food and transportation, you'll have no other expenses."

The children were ecstatic. They gladly joined their parents in making even more sacrifices for the train fares.

In Bretagne, Yo-Yo and Yeou-Cheng enjoyed running along the seashore, kicking waves along the way, swimming to their hearts' content, picking shells and keeping up their music practice.

Brother and sister met other children on the beach — the only place they played with them. Never at home. The house was a place to study not to play. Intrusion by other children was seldom permitted except when they came to play chamber music with Yo-Yo and Yeou-Cheng.

It was not difficult to sense the importance Marina placed on their lifestyle. The Mas were no ordinary people; they had forged ahead by the strength of their moral values, their strong family bonds, and their extraordinary music talents. Playtime for the children had its limitations. There were other more important ways to expend their energies.

Chinese culture was as important to the Mas as Western culture, neither was to be neglected. Besides French, which became second nature to the two children, Yo-Yo and Yeou-Cheng spoke Chinese at

Vacationing in Bretagne. Marina and her two children.

A happy Yo-Yo sailing his boat on the shores of Brittany.

home and were taught by their father to write Chinese characters. Two hours of meticulous planning went into a lesson that took ten minutes for the children to master. Dr. Ma used the same method of teaching a language as he did for music, progressing a little at a time, first one character, then three, then five, and so on until an entire lesson had been mastered. As Yo-Yo and Yeou-Cheng grew older, their father insisted that they keep a diary in Chinese to further reinforce their command of the language and keep alive their heritage to remind them who and what they were.

Who and what Yo-Yo should be, however, was not always clear to him until his more mature years, when, like his father, he became his own best critic. Then and only then was he able to appreciate his father's strict discipline and the demands he made on himself and on those he taught. This sentiment was expressed by Yo-Yo in a newspaper interview when he was a young man, "Both my parents encouraged me to have standards of my own — to develop them as much as I could, and not to believe in compliments but to know always how I stand with myself, with my own conscience."[4]

These happy memories flashed through Marina's mind as she stood in front of that house in Ormesson, unmindful of what her husband and his friend were saying until she heard Dr. Ma addressing her, "Well, what do you think? Maybe I should consult my brother about this?"

"Maybe your brother will think we are both crazy," she retorted. She was wrong.

To her surprise, the brother not only encouraged them to go through with the purchase — he sent them the down payment, adding that the carrying charges and taxes could be covered from his salary at the Trent School.

With the school contract now in his hands, Dr. Ma proceeded to buy the house.

Moving from their old apartment was a lot of work, but it was fun too. The entire family set themselves to the task of making their home livable, putting off major repair work for a later date. Their attention was now turned to getting ready for their imminent departure.

"Oh, Mommy, if we could only move this house to New York," the children kept repeating.

By a quirk of fate, however, their joy almost came to a disastrous end.

---

4. *The Christian Science Monitor,* 26 May 1978.

13. Prelude to Manhattan

The sun that had been shining on the garden side of the house now moved toward the back and a slight breeze swayed the branches of the fruit trees. Inside, Yo-Yo and Yeou-Cheng were practicing their music. At one point, Yo-Yo laid his cello aside and walked toward a window on the far end of the room facing the garden to allow a breath of cool air into the stuffy room. Without even lifting her head from the music score, Yeou-Cheng called out to him, "Leave the window alone. Don't bother opening it. Get back to your music. You know what Daddy told us, 'Never interrupt your practice, it makes you lose concentration, the flow and the mood.'"

"How will he know? He's not home. You always worry too much." And he proceeded to open the window, which was stuck. As he applied greater pressure, the fragile glass pane broke into pieces and one of them cut deep into Yo-Yo's wrist. He let out a loud cry of pain. Blood began flowing freely. Before Yeou-Cheng could go to his aid, his mother, who was in the adjoining room, leaped to his side. "Yo-Yo, Yo-Yo, what have you done?"

Quick to realize the dire consequences this accident could have on his career, Marina tied his upper arm with a piece of cloth in a frantic effort to stop the bleeding. Then, taking Yo-Yo by the hand, she ran to a neighbour's house for help. Her son, she pleaded, had to be rushed to the hospital.

By sheer luck, her neighbour, a cab driver, happened to be home.

"Oh, Madame, I am desolate, but I cannot drive you to the hospital. You see, I have to follow stupid company rules. The hospital is located outside our zone....I cannot break the rules...*Je suis désolé*, Madame — I'm so sorry."

Marina panicked. Though the bleeding had slowed down some-
what, she felt helpless. Her son needed immediate medical attention
and she didn't know where to turn.

By chance, another neighbour, who happened to see Marina rush
out of her house, came running over. He put mother and son into his
car and drove to the emergency room.

"You're a mighty lucky boy," the doctor told Yo-Yo. Then turning
to Marina, "You came in the nick of time; had you delayed, your son
would have suffered permanent injuries to his arm. He's a very, very
lucky boy," the doctor repeated.

Days later, when Dr. Ma related the incident to Monsieur Vatelot,
the *lutier*, the latter expressed relief.

"The accident could have put an end to Yo-Yo's career even before
he got started."

With the exception of this incident, the Mas had nothing
but pleasant memories of Ormesson. And they did return there
for their vacations to enjoy the peace and quiet of their little *pied-
à-terre* admiring the beautiful flowers and picking fruit from the
trees.

During one of his sojourns in Ormesson, Dr. Ma expressed his
happy feelings in a letter to his friend, John A. Rallo:

Cher Ami,
...N'oubliez pas: lorsque vous viendrez en Europe, Ormesson est aussi
votre pied-à-terre. Une nouvelle chambre et un nouveau salon vous
attendent déjà pour vous recevoir. Sachez que depuis deux ans j'ai bien
améliorer des installations: un chauffe-eau éléctrique donne
instantanément de l'eau très chaude en abondance. Deux lits et deux
matelas neufs sont à votre disposition. De grands placards, penderie et
étagères et des tiroirs pour ranger vos affaires. Un Steinway et deux cents
partitions d'opéras attendent votre femme pour qu'elle reprenne sa voix
de chanteresse.
    Au marché, il y a toujours des truites que vous aimez (et dont j'enlèverai
la peau avant de vous servir). Et il y a aussi des crevettes vivantes tous les
samedis. Et puis vous aurez des fleurs, des fruits et des légumes frais dans
le jardin qui sera mieux entretenu.

Soyez bienvenus à tout moment.[5]

Imperceptibly, the calendar pages had turned and classes were due to start at the Trent School. The Mas were finally ready for their departure and for a new life in New York City.

While looking for a permanent residence, they stayed at a West Side hotel. A month later, they found an apartment at 16 Madison Avenue, where they met the Zabriskies and to whom they were drawn close since they shared a mutual love of music and a background of French language and culture.

---

5.   Dear Friend,
    ...Don't forget: when you come to Europe, Ormesson will also be your *pied-à-terre.* A new bedroom and a new living room are ready for you. I want you to know that several improvements have been made in the last two years: a hot water heater provides instantly all the hot water you want. You will have two beds and two mattresses for your convenience. Large closets, a pantry, shelves and drawers for all your things. A Steinway and two hundred opera excerpts await your wife so that she can practice her singing.
    At the market, one may always find trout, which you like so much (I'll remove the skin before serving you). Live shrimp is available every Saturday. Then, you will have flowers, fruits and fresh vegetables from the garden which has been well-maintained.
    You will be welcome at any time.

14. Too High, Too Low

Tall, handsome and gentle-mannered, John Zabriskie, M.D. was married to a French-born woman whose gracious personality shone through her warm smile. Their three wonderful children: John, Christopher and Valerie were enrolled in Dr. Ma's music classes. Engaged full-time in cancer research at Rockefeller University, Dr. Zabriskie had three passions: family, medical research and music.

It was natural for him to be eager to take cello lessons with such a masterful instructor, but he wondered whether Dr. Ma would accept an adult student.

"Of course, *avec plaisir* — with pleasure. Music is for people of all ages." Then added, "Provided that you take your studies seriously if you want results.

The young scientist gave his promise…and kept it, practicing each lesson religiously.

During one of the sessions, Dr. Zabriskie sat facing his instructor, who had his back to the corridor. From that position, Dr. Ma could not see Yo-Yo standing near the door, his ears glued to the notes coming out of the cello.

At one point, as was customary, Dr. Ma decided to test his student's awareness of pitch.

"That note you're playing," he asked, "is it too high or too low?"

Dr. Zabriskie was caught off guard; he wasn't sure; but he did not wish to disappoint the instructor with the wrong answer. As he looked up, he caught sight of Yo-Yo, who signaled to him by pointing a long finger upwards.

"Too high," the doctor blurted out putting his trust in the boy's expertise.

"Good," said the pleased instructor and asked him to play another note.

"And that one, is it too high or too low?"

Dr. Zabriskie's eyes quickly shifted to the corridor: Yo-Yo's finger was pointing downward.

"Too low," he answered with self-assurance.

"Remarkable!" exclaimed the delighted teacher with a great feeling of satisfaction. "You have a good ear." And then he proceeded with the rest of the lesson.

By the time Dr. Ma found out the source of his student's competence, the Zabriskies and the Mas had become good friends, and whenever they recalled the "too high, too low episode," they never failed to laugh over the doctor's "good musical ear."

15. Pablo Casals

When Alexander Schneider of the famed Budapest Quartet first made the acquaintance of the Mas, he never thought for a moment that the little "pipsqueak" standing before him was a music genius in the making. Then he heard him play.

He marvelled at the boy's long fingers gliding along with measured restraint, his eyes never looking down at the fingerboard. His concentration was unwavering, as his bow, making contact with the strings, drew out the most delicious tones.

When it was over, he shook his head in unbelieving admiration. "Bravo!" he exclaimed. He could not think of any other words for the moment, so moved was he. And almost in the same breath, turning to Dr. Ma, "Has Pablo heard him play?"

He was referring to Pablo Casals, the internationally acclaimed cello master.

"No, he hasn't."

"Well, I think he should. I'll speak to him. He used to live three floors above you, in this apartment building. Did you know that?"

"No," Hiao-Tsiun answered, "I had no way of knowing that."

True to his word, Alexander Schneider lost no time in arranging a meeting with the venerable, Catalán-born cellist. The "audition" took place in Casals' own music room in the hotel where he was now living.

Marina remembered looking at all the scuff marks made on the wooden floor by Casals' cello end pin — intricate, indecipherable, silent designs that told of the many hours the maestro spent practicing.

When the audition was over, Casals picked up Yo-Yo and sat him on his lap. "Would you like to play some more?" he asked routinely, thinking that the boy would be tired after his performance.

He should have known better. For Yo-Yo, the playing had just begun.

"Yes, yes," he answered beaming with such genuine excitement that the maestro just leaned back in his chair and listened as Yo-Yo's bow "sang."

But as he listened, charmed by the child's performance, his mind was busy searching for a way to expose the bespectacled "wonder boy" to a wider audience.

By chance, he glanced at a table next to him. There, on top of a pile of music sheets, lay a letter he had recently received. He was being informed that Leonard Bernstein[6] was to conduct a televised program, "The American Pageant of the Arts," to kick off a fund-raising campaign for Washington's Cultural Center.

"That's it!" The maestro had found the open door he was looking for. He would ask Bernstein to include Yo-Yo on the program.

---

6. It is interesting to note that, just a few hours before his death (14 October 1990) Bernstein, who had helped launch Yo-Yo on his career, was found sitting before a T.V. set, reportedly watching a concert given by Yo-Yo.

16. An Invitation to Kennedy Center

The televised "The American Pageant of the Arts" won nation-wide acclaim. As a result of this appearance, Yo-Yo was among several luminaries, including Pablo Casals, who were invited to participate in the gala benefit concert scheduled to be held at the Washington National Armory, on 29 November 1962, featuring Leonard Bernstein as Master of Ceremonies.

Marina could scarcely contain her emotions; only her eyes revealed the depth of her pride. She could hardly believe what was happening. After all, Yo-Yo was only seven years old, and Yeou-Cheng, who was to accompany him at the piano, was only eleven. There was no doubt that the parents were more anxious than their children. To appear together with so many world-famous people! And before the President of the United States and his wife!

Jacqueline Kennedy had brought an aura of elegance in style and speech to Washington. In the wake of the lusterless receptions and ceremonial events held at the White House mansion during the Eisenhower administration, she was a fresh breath endeavouring to turn the nation's capital into a cultural centre. According to her own husband and his close advisers, she was a most desirable asset to his Presidency. Her type of glamour was precisely what the nation needed at that time.

Just before the concert, Yo-Yo seemed a bit nervous. It was not at all like him to be that way.

"Are you scared?" his father asked.

"A little."

"What are you scared of? You know your music perfectly well."

"It's not that. It's that…"

"The large size of the audience, perhaps?" Five thousand people were expected to attend.

"Oh, no. Not that. It's just that my cello is small and I'm scared that the sound will not be loud enough for all those people to hear."

His father chuckled and reassured him, "Don't worry about that, there will be loud speakers."

Armed with his customary self-confidence, Yo-Yo went on to give an outstanding performance, sharing the thunderous applause with his sister.

The following day, *The Washington Post* carried rave reviews. A photo of him holding a cello appeared on the same page, side by side, with three photos of the First Lady.

Such publicity would have filled an ordinary child's head with ideas of grandeur. But not Yo-Yo. The raves, the applause, the adulation did nothing to inflate his ego; but it did make him feel

Yo-Yo and Yeou-Cheng being congratulated by Maestro Leonard Bernstein after the Kennedy Benefit Concert in Washington, D.C.

Maestro Leonard Bernstein posing for a photograph
with the young musicians.

accepted for what he was, for what he was sharing with the audience.
His little heart was regenerated, replenished as he became even more
aware of the difficult road that lay ahead. Henceforth, he would work
even harder to master his instrument, to make those strings "sing out"
the music as he felt it within his soul.

My Parents
My parents taught me to believe in the soul,
in that something extra, in the beauty that
is in human nature.

— Yo-Yo

My Father
My father taught me the language of music,
The value of time, and the bonds of friendship.
He pointed out to me the first buds of Spring,
The wonders of nature, and the meaning of words.

My father gave me courage, taught me patience,
Determination and pride in our heritage;
He read to me geography, history and other stories.
A man of few words, he taught by his silence.

— Yeou-Cheng

17. A Bond of Friendship

The Trent School building soon became too small to accommodate the large number of pupils requesting admission, and it was sold to the Day School of the Church of the Heavenly Rest. Most of the Trent students and staff joined the École Française de New York — a bilingual school with classes through grade 5 — on East 62nd Street and Madison Ave.

Hiao-Tsiun Ma continued his teaching and direction of the Children's Orchestra at the École Française de New York. On 17 December, 1964, the parents of that institution's *élèves* put on a fundraising benefit at Carnegie Hall.

"The new school doesn't pose a problem for Yo-Yo," Marina remarked to her husband, "since he is going into the fifth grade. As for Yeou-Cheng, she is registered at the Brearley School."

To prepare for the eventual establishment of a high school, John A. Rallo, formerly of the Lycée Français de New York, was selected to serve as Director-Designate.

Hiao-Tsiun Ma and John A. Rallo had many things in common. Both were heirs of ancient cultures: the one Chinese, the other Trinacrian.[7] Both shared an adopted heritage of French language and culture. Both had been brought up along traditional lines with emphasis on duty, honour, discipline, family values, hard work, and individualism. It was natural for the two to cement a lifelong friendship.

The École Française prospered...for a time. Before long, however,

---

7. Sicilian. Trinacria was the ancient name of Sicily.

it became evident that the direction of the school was not fulfilling the aspirations of the two educators, and that the proposed high school would not materialize. Moreover, the manner in which the Director carried out policies conflicted with the ethical principles of the two men, resulting in their resignation from their respective positions in May 1967.

Dr. Rallo returned to his home in Connecticut, where he continued to work in the field of foreign language education. Dr. Ma opened his own studio, giving private lessons to children from various schools and founding his own Children's Orchestra, with Yo-Yo and Yeou-Cheng as principal cellist and violinist. The Rallo children, John-Peter and Christopher, continued as fledgling musicians in that orchestra.

The dream Dr. Ma had first envisioned in that one-room apartment in Paris was finally a reality. The splendid annual concerts the

The Ma Family (1963).

Children's Orchestra performed in the Caspary Hall auditorium at Rockefeller University vindicated the belief in his method of teaching, convinced as he was that children learn best "by making music together."

As he lowered the baton at the end of each performance, he could smile inwardly with pride that his two children had contributed so significantly to his achievement. While his own personal dream had been realized, he looked far into the future when his gifted Yo-Yo would make his mark as an international cellist.

Thursday Evening, December 17, 1964, at 8:30 o'clock

PARENTS
OF
THE ÉCOLE FRANÇAISE

in

An Evening at Carnegie Hall

Diahann Carroll	*Harold Rome*
Phyllis Curtin	*Arthur Schwartz*
George Gaynes	*Isaac Stern*
Alan Jay Lerner	*Maria Tallchief*

Julius Rudel
and
THE NEW YORK CITY CENTER ORCHESTRA

Mozart	Overture to "The Marriage of Figaro"
	Julius Rudel *conducting the Orchestra*
H. T. Ma	Hommage à Bach *(for Orchestra)*
	Allegretto
	Allegro
	Allegretto
Joseph Strimer	"Biniou," French Dance *(for Orchestra)*
Arranged and Orchestrated by *H. T. Ma*	**Dr. H. T. Ma** *conducting the Orchestra*
G. B. Sammartini	Sonata in G Major for Cello and Piano
	1st Movement: Allegro
	Yo-Yo Ma, *Cello*
	Yeou-Cheng Ma, *Piano*
	"Two Tin Soldiers"
Ambroise Thomas	*Air du tambour major* from *"Le Caïd"*
Gilbert & Sullivan	*Private Willis' Song* from *"Iolanthe"*
	George Gaynes, *Bass-Baritone*

(Continued on following page)

(Continued from preceding page)

Massenet	Scene and Gavotte from *"Manon"*
Johann Strauss	Czardas from *"Die Fledermaus"*
	Phyllis Curtin, *Soprano*
Saint-Saëns	Introduction and Rondo capriccioso
	Isaac Stern, *Violin*

INTERMISSION

Villa-Lobos	*La Campagnarde du Brésil* from *Suite pour Chant et Violon*
	Phyllis Curtin and Isaac Stern
Tchaikovsky	*Pas de Deux* from Act II of *Swan Lake*
	Maria Tallchief and André Prokovsky
	Isaac Stern, *Violin Solo*
	ALAN JAY LERNER, HAROLD ROME, and ARTHUR SCHWARTZ play LERNER, ROME, and SCHWARTZ
Rodgers & Hart	Little Girl Blue
	Diahann Carroll

18. Learning with Lightning Speed

With Yo-Yo enrolled at Trinity School, Dr. Ma was now able to turn his attention to finding a cello instructor for his son. After much consideration, he entrusted Yo-Yo to the noted cellist, Janos Scholz. Within two short years, thanks to his prodigious memory, the "boy wonder" had mastered such an impressive repertoire that he astonished even his well-seasoned teacher, who spoke of his pupil with candid fondness as the boy "who learned with lightning speed."

The time had come for Yo-Yo to study with another teacher.

Isaac Stern, one of the foremost violinists, had heard Yo-Yo play in Paris when the boy was only five years old. Even then he sensed that Yo-Yo, almost dwarfed by the size of his cello, was an astonishingly gifted child, "one of the brightest talents to come along in many years." Now that Yo-Yo was nearing the age of nine, the Russian-born violinist, familiar throughout the world as a "champion of cultural preservation in America," thought it was time to ask his friend and chamber music ensemble performer, Leonard Rose, to take Yo-Yo under his wing.

The American-born cellist, whom Arturo Toscanini had engaged to play in the NBC Symphony Orchestra as assistant first cello-player, at the age of twenty-five had joined the New York Philharmonic as solo cellist. As a faculty member of the Juilliard College, he undoubtedly harboured the secret hope that one of his students might one day take his place among the world's great cellists. He was delighted to have such a remarkable student as Yo-Yo. Rose's dream came true later for, as he told an interviewer, "One of my pupils, in particular, is one of the greatest cellists in the world."[8] Of course, he was referring to Yo-Yo.

The maestro quickly understood his protégé's aspirations and realized that he had to allow him a great deal of leeway in the interpretation of master works. Eventually, in spite of their age difference, the two became good friends. The elder cellist adopted a paternal attitude toward his pupil, nourishing and enriching and admiring him. During an interview with Richard Thorne, Leonard Rose said, "By the time Yo-Yo was eleven or twelve, I had already taken him through the most difficult études. He may have one of the greatest techniques of all time. I'm always floored by it."

Leonard Rose may have been "floored" by Yo-Yo's technique, but to Marina Ma, who had closely supervised her son's development, it was but a consequence of his home environment. Thanks to his father's analytical, technical and intellectual approach to music and to his mother's subtle suggestion not to neglect the emotional effect, Yo-Yo's cello ceased to be a mere instrument with a voice box — it became an extension of his own body and soul.

Like the cello pin marks on the floor which had borne witness to Pablo Casals' "effort and pain," sculptor-like, Marina's son carved out "every single thing" with similar "effort and pain."

---

8.   Marjorie Barrett, *Rocky Mountain News*, Denver, Colorado, 25 January 1974.

19. The Cello Has a Voice

arina loved to listen to Schubert's *Sonata*, which Yo-Yo and Yeou-Cheng often played by themselves. "It's such a lovely piece — not to be played by a child, by any means," she said. "It has strong, powerful emotions that seasoned performers can understand. But not youngsters. It's entirely too difficult."

In spite of Marina's perceptions, one of Leonard Rose's assistant teachers at Juilliard College suggested that brother and sister play it together.

One afternoon, as Yo-Yo was rehearsing his part, Marina entered the room and quietly listened to his playing. Suddenly he stopped, looked up at his mother, and out of the clear blue sky asked her to sing.

"Sing?" she said, taken entirely by surprise by the unexpected request. "Sing what?"

"The *Sonata*."

Although still puzzled why he wanted her to sing, she complied. There must be a good reason, she thought, for Yo-Yo to ask.

When she finished singing, Yo-Yo turned to her, "How come you can make it and I can't?"

At first Marina was perplexed by the meaning of his words. Upon reflecting she understood.

"Yo-Yo, my son," she replied, "remember you are still very young. You haven't yet perfected your technique. What you want to show with your cello is what a practiced singer can do with her voice. A singer does it naturally. The voice is in her, in her little box." And she pointed to her throat. "It is a natural voice, very natural." To show the emotion of the *Sonata*, you have to master the right phrasing along with perfect technique. A good singer can make it because of her natural voice. She is born with that gift. To move people, she must project special feelings that cannot be expressed by words alone. They must come from within. That's the way she can interpret and express the mood the composer wishes to create.

Striving for that delicate point of technique that gives the cello a voice.

"A cellist or violinist needs to acquire the technique to pour out his feelings. But when a good singer sings, listeners feel comfortable. She doesn't stop to think how it's done. It's just there, but it's not easy. It takes a lot of practice, but it's easier than trying to achieve the same result with a cello."

As she spoke, Marina recalled earlier days when she used to sing opera at the Paris Conservatory. But as she focused her attention on her young son's sad face, she added a word of consolation, "Maybe in a year or two you'll understand better how to reach that point of technique."

His mother's words left a deep impression on the boy. Indeed, it did take a few years of hard work, but he finally reached that delicate point that she had described.

When he played, he could listen to himself and hear that inner voice reverberating. His bow sang the notes, drawing out a range of human emotions, as it made contact with the strings and brought out marvellous sounds. At that moment, music became a human expression.

20. Toward the Exclusive Circle

Six years had passed since the Mas had gone to Berkeley, California to visit Marina's sister.

"I think we can afford another trip," Hiao-Tsiun told his wife. "It will be good for the children to see their aunt again now that they're older."

When they got there, they learned that the news of the twelve-year old Yo-Yo's musical talent had preceded him, and he was asked to appear with the San Francisco Little Symphony.

Of this performance, Arthur Bloomfield, music critic for the *Examiner* reported:

> Would you believe me if I wrote that a bespectacled 12 year-old boy came on stage yesterday and played the cello so startlingly well that he must be counted in the same category as Starker, Rose, Varga, Piatigorsky, and Casals? Well, it's the truth.[9]

Raising a gifted child was both a blessing and a burden of responsibility for the Mas, but they held fast to their conviction that Destiny had traced a path for Yo-Yo to follow — an unmarked path that would lead him to that exclusive circle reserved for the handful of *virtuosi*.

Being part of that circle was going to have its drawbacks. Requests for Yo-Yo to make public appearances poured in. Many a child prodigy's career had fallen by the wayside as a result of over-exposure to gain public acclaim. Dr. Ma knew that. In his role as Yo-Yo's

---

9. *San Francisco Examiner*, 28 October 1968.

"manager," he followed the same pedagogical principle he had applied in teaching music: letting a pupil proceed a little at a time until the technique became second nature to him. He limited his son's engagements so that an audience, having been exposed to Yo-Yo's staggering ability would clamour for more. This paced exposure allowed Yo-Yo more time to discipline himself in order to reach that musical ideal, that

Being a cellist is no easy task.

spiritual coming together between a composer's intention and the artist's rendition.

Contrary to Oscar Wilde's assertion that "nothing succeeds like excess," Dr. Ma's wisdom prevailed. In looking back he could smile at himself as he recalled the time he had told Marina when Yo-Yo was two years old that his son had such a poor memory, that he was a little good for nothing and that he would never amount to anything.

21. The Burning Grass

Music was not the only concern for Marina in raising her son. She made sure Yo-Yo's health and well-being were safeguarded, for he was a typically normal, restless boy.

When he appeared on the stage as a child prodigy, audiences marvelled at him as a performer, but there was a human side, a personal side which varied little from other boys his age in many respects. Like them he could be an adventurer, but unlike them he was forbidden to engage in any activity that might injure his hands.

Twelve-year old boys like to sleep late in the morning; mothers know that only too well. Yo-Yo was no exception. In vain Marina would try to get him out of bed: "Yo-Yo, wake up, it's 6:00 a.m.

"Mmmmm. Oh, Mom!"

Fifteen minutes passed and Yo-Yo was still in bed.

"Yo-Yo, wake up! It's late."

This time, Marina shook him out of his slumber.

"O.K., Mom. I'll be up in a minute." But the warmth of the bed was too good to abandon, and he buried his face deeper into the pillow.

Silence from the sleeping boy would prompt Marina to go to his room and throw aside the covers. That always worked.

For a half hour before breakfast, Yo-Yo routinely practiced his cello, while his mother prepared toast or pancakes or Chinese food, which he enjoyed eating early in the morning. Then off he went to Trinity, the school he attended after the École Française.

In the afternoon, after classes, Marina always had snacks and refreshments for him — he looked particularly forward to a drink of cool grape juice, rich in vitamin C. One hour of cello practice was followed by two or more hours of homework or writing his daily diary in Chinese. Family dinner was at 7:00 p.m.

For after-dinner relaxation, Yo-Yo looked at T.V. for a half hour: "Little House on the Prairie" and "Daniel Boone" were among his favourite programs.

So much did he look forward to this diversion, that his father used it as a means of punishment — besides the usual *bonne fessée* — a good slap on the behind — whenever Yo-Yo misbehaved.

The television set was in the dining room and Dr. Ma's place at table faced it with his back toward the door of the kitchen to which Yo-Yo was sent when he was punished. Yo-Yo, however, often managed to evade the punishment by making sure he left the door ajar so he could peek through the opening.

Marina was aware of Yo-Yo's inventiveness but never let on, praying that her husband would not turn around.

The rest of the evening was devoted to homework, reviewing for tests, or supplementary music practice, with bedtime between 9:30 p.m. and 10:00 p.m. At age twelve, Yo-Yo was allowed an additional hour to 11:00 p.m. It was not unusual for him, especially when he had only two weeks to memorize a sonata, to spend this extra time for more intensive practice.

The Mas occupied an apartment on the fifth floor of a building on East 94th Street. Dr. Ma's studio, where he gave private music lessons, was located two floors below his family residence. It was in this studio that Yo-Yo practiced in the evening, next to the room where his father sometimes slept.

Half asleep, half awake, Hiao-Tsiun listened to his son's playing, and whenever he heard an inexact note, he would tell Yo-Yo to play it again and again until it was perfect. To avoid his father's criticism, the boy played very softly so as not to awaken him. Marina maintained tongue in cheek, "That's why his *pianissimos* are so brilliant."

To give her children enough fresh air and exercise, she used to take them to Central Park, where Yo-Yo romped on the grass and climbed huge boulders.

One sunny afternoon, she was seated on a bench chatting with Yeou-Cheng, while, not too far from her, Yo-Yo played behind some of the big rocks. Suddenly Marina saw flames shooting up. "Oh, *mon*

Dieu! — heavens above! — my Yo-Yo's there. She panicked and rushed to the scene. There was her son unharmed, calmly watching the spreading fire fanned by the light breeze. She stood there not knowing what to do and was about to shout for help, when three young men rushed to the scene and, to her great relief, extinguished the flames.

When calm was restored, Marina turned to Yo-Yo, "Did you have anything to do with that fire?" She remembered that one of her son's classmates had casually mentioned that he used to have matches in his pocket.

Yo-Yo was forthright in his answer, "Mom, I lit the dry grass just to have some fun. I didn't think of the danger. When I saw the fire, I didn't know how to put it out. Then the flames started to spread and I got scared."

"Yo-Yo," the mother warned, "you know I must tell your father about this."

Yo-Yo felt shivers running down his spine. He knew he deserved to be punished, yet...

"Mom, please," he pleaded, "please don't tell Dad."

Marina was torn between her sense of justice and her maternal instinct to shield her young. She looked at him sternly.

"But if I don't tell your father, how do I know you will not do it again?"

"I promise you, Mom. I promise you. I'll never do it again," he bleated with the innocence of a lamb.

She relented but added, "Don't ever let it happen again, otherwise I'll be forced to tell your father not only about this incident but also about other misdeeds I have not previously reported to him."

"Oh, Mom, thank you, thank you." Yo-Yo remained true to his word and his father never knew what had happened behind that boulder in Central Park.

"Poor Daddy," Marina told the Rallos who, by this time had become close friends, "he never found out. I didn't have the heart to tell him. He gets so upset when his son misbehaves." Then she added half-seriously, "That's why my hair started turning gray faster than my husband's."

In spite of her graying hair, Marina never looked her age, and when she spoke, there was always a youthful timber to her voice.

"Yo-Yo was always a real boy, always full of fun. We didn't allow our children to have too many friends or to participate in too many outside activities. My Yo-Yo and Yeou-Cheng had no time for that. In America there are always so many goings on: school functions, parties, hours spent on the telephone, to say nothing of involvement in sports. My children had very little free time. School work, music lessons, Chinese and French studies kept them well occupied." Then, on a philosophical note, she added, "I think parents try to mold their children in their own image. Is it good or is it bad? Who can tell. Maybe parents are out of tune with changing times, but in the long run, good, solid values are for all ages. Parents can only do what they think is best for their children according to their own consciences. As a child, Yo-Yo understood our ways and what we were trying to accomplish, and he went along. But as he grew older, well…"

22. A Day to Remember

Summertime! Schools were closed and with most of the children away on vacation, the Mas could afford to spend a few days in the Connecticut home of the Rallos. House visits between the two families had become more frequent: the Mas enjoyed Italian food, while the Rallos developed a taste for Chinese cuisine expertly prepared Cantonese style by Marina or Szechwan by Hiao-Tsiun himself.

After serving the main meal at 1:00 p.m. — the customary European dinner time — hosts and guests were enjoying a cup of tea, which Dr. Ma had brought back from a trip to Hong Kong. Yeou-Cheng, by this time in her mid-teens, remained with the adults, while Yo-Yo was allowed to go down to the basement playroom with Christopher, the younger of the two Rallo sons.

Judging from the noise heard upstairs, there was no doubt that whatever the boys were doing was getting out of hand and that intervention was necessary. Fearful that Dr. Ma might blame his son for the raucous behaviour, Dr. Rallo rushed to the scene before his friend had a chance to say anything, and found the two boys swinging Tarzan-like from the water and heating pipes. He roared directly at Christopher to get down at once but spared Yo-Yo from embarrassment. The culprits bolted like a shot to the second floor bedroom, seeking sanctuary. There, they were joined by John-Peter, the quiet one.

Dr. Rallo thought that the boys' energies had been spent and that his roar had produced the intended effect. He was dead wrong.

The ceiling above the dining room began shaking as if a mild earthquake had struck. The crystal chandelier over the table began to oscillate rhythmically. More trouble! Dr. Rallo ran upstairs and wildly swung the door open. There they were, red-faced, his two sons having the time of their lives with a pillow fight against Yo-Yo. Once again he chided Christopher directly, accusing him of instigating the trouble, while shielding Yo-Yo from the blame. Before he had finished, however, the three scrambled for the doorway and made a dash for the outdoors.

Seeing the camouflaged mortification on Dr. Ma's face, Dr. Rallo made light of the matter, reminding his guest that "boys will be boys" and that they have to get rid of their excessive energies. Tension was broken, and peace and tranquillity reigned at last.

A note Yo-Yo sent sometime later brought out his natural disposition towards fairness and his irrepressible sense of humour:

Let's do it right, this time around. Yo-Yo looks over Chris' shoulder, while John-Peter plays on.

Dear Dr. Rallo, Mrs. Rallo and Family,

   I would like to say "thank you" for including me as a member of your family during my stay there, but then it would not be true, for even though at times I felt as if I were a member of the family, you did not treat me as one; if I remember correctly, not once was I told to do anything, not once was I scolded, and besides, I did not succeed once in trying to argue with anyone. So, regretfully, I must say "thank you all" for having me staying over and "thank you" for having made me very happy and full.

With much love,
Yo-Yo

On a subsequent visit to the Rallos, another adventure took place.

Close to their Connecticut residence, there was a river. Though it is polluted now, it had not always been so. Christopher loved to fish in its waters abundantly stocked with trout. When Dr. Ma heard Christopher inviting Yo-Yo to go fishing, he became quite alarmed. The possibility that a fishing hook could cause serious damage to his son's hands was enough for him to issue a stern order, "Yo-Yo you are not to play around with fishing hooks under any circumstances. They are too dangerous for you."

Christopher understood Dr. Ma's concern, but youngsters quite often act without regard to consequences. Seeing the disappointment in his friend's eyes, he felt sorry. But Yo-Yo said nothing; he was used to being deprived from engaging in certain sports that might put an end to his career.

"May we go for a walk in the park?" Chris asked Dr. Ma.

"Now, that's a good idea," he replied. "The exercise will do both of you good."

Christopher's father took his son aside and warned further, "Chris, don't you dare pull one of your tricks. Be careful."

The two boys walked to the park, along the northern side which bordered on the river. There was Jim, one of Chris' friends, casting his fishing rod into the rushing stream. Chris' eyes brightened. "Yo-Yo," he said, "I have a plan. I can borrow Jim's rod, bait the hook and hand it over to you. When a fish bites, the rod will bend; you reel in the line

Fishing in the river.

and hand it over to me. I'll do the rest. You'll never touch the hook and we'll keep our promise to our parents."

That day was a memorable one for Yo-Yo, who experienced the pleasure of "going fishing."

Dr. Ma never suspected the escape hatch which the two friends had concocted. It was neither the first nor was it going to be the last time that Yo-Yo's little escapades would remain a secret.

23. Good-bye to the "Y"

A t last! The long-awaited Spring break at Radcliffe College and a chance for Yeou-Cheng to get away from her books and a rigorous pre-med schedule. She had found precious little time to devote herself to her first love: the violin, and she looked forward to a reunion with her family and the luxury of practicing her music without external pressures.

She had always been close to Yo-Yo and had kept fully informed about the minutest details of his daily activities. Today was Friday, one of the most anticipated days of the week for her brother, who was supposed to go swimming at the "Y." But he wasn't getting ready, and she wondered why. Swimming provided the relaxation and therapy he so much needed for his arm and back muscles; it was a sure way of ridding himself of his frustrations. That was one physical activity for which Yo-Yo needed neither reminders nor prodding, so great was the enjoyment he derived from going to the "Y."

Was her brother in some kind of trouble? Was he suffering from some ailment barring him from physical exercise, which he did not want to reveal to his parents? They always worried so. This was not the time for guessing games, and she decided to ask him outright.

"No, Sis, nothing's the matter. I'm fine. It's just that I've lost interest in it. Nothing else," he told her matter-of-factly.

Yeou-Cheng knew her brother only too well to believe this simple explanation, but she let the matter drop. Perhaps her mother knew.

Marina had no answer. "When I asked him if he was going to the "Y" this morning, he flatly told me 'no.' And he also told me that he would not be going there any more." She paused thoughtfully. "Daddy doesn't know. Don't you breathe a word to him about this."

Deep in her heart, Yeou-Cheng knew her brother would not have given up swimming on a whim. She pressed him to tell her the truth. "Yo-Yo," she began in her usual, sisterly way, "you've always confided in me. You know I can be trusted. Tell me what really did happen?"

Yeou-Cheng devotes herself to her first love: the violin (Caspary Hall, Rockefeller Center. Rehearsing for the Children's Orchestra Concert.)

It was not so much for lack of trust but for embarrassment that he hesitated. But then, the real reason would eventually come out. Besides, she had always been his confidante.

At the pool, two gays had laid eyes on his slender, muscular, Oriental body as he swam his laps. They kept a close watch on him in the locker room. Undoubtedly, his friendly smile and personal charm had attracted them to him. They may even have mistaken that smile. Yo-Yo had always been an extremely friendly person. In the past few weeks they seemed to be wherever Yo-Yo was. The fifteen-year old youth, though completely oblivious to the physical attraction he stirred in them, thought they were just trying to be sociable until one day, when he found himself alone in the locker room with one of the two men.

The stranger watched Yo-Yo as he toweled himself, his gray eyes glued to the youthful body. For the first time, Yo-Yo felt uneasy. Hurriedly, he slipped into his trousers without daring to look up. When he did lift his head, he saw the stranger standing right before him. Yo-Yo did not allow him to say a single word; he had clearly understood the man's intentions. Frightened and at the same time filled with disgust, he grabbed the rest of his clothes and made a dash for the exit door, vowing never again to go swimming at the "Y."

Ignorant of what had taken place, Marina was distressed over the entire affair especially since the required annual fee had been paid in full with no hope for even a partial refund. She thought that her son was unreasonable and even lazy. After all, they didn't have money to waste.

In time, when she finally learned the truth, she regretted accusing Yo-Yo of laziness and understood his reluctance and embarrassment to discuss the matter with her.

As on previous occasions, she never told her husband about it, deeming it prudent to keep the incident to herself.

24. About Critics and Reviews

T he living room window of the Mas' fifth floor apartment offered a wide view of the sky. As Marina was looking out from behind the glass pane, she caught a glimpse of a solitary bird flying low, dashing across the window, then with quickened flaps of the wings soaring into the blue. She strained to catch a last look at its flight before it disappeared completely from sight. "Children are so much like birds," she sighed, "they don't like to be caged."

It made her think of the story of a man who had a parakeet named Figaro. He used to let it out of the cage to flit about the high-ceilinged room. The little creature acquired the habit of swooping down onto the man's shoulder and nibbling affectionately at his ear. The man, who lived alone, felt good; he loved the comfort he derived from his feathered friend.

One summer day the man went for a drive in the country taking Figaro along. "I wonder what would happen if I gave him a taste of freedom?" he thought. Opening the door to the cage he coaxed the bird to come out. Hesitant at first, little by little Figaro took flight. He flew high, then low, then in circles, finally disappearing in the distance. The man was disappointed at seeing the bird fly away. Would he come back? he wondered.

Sunset approached and Figaro was nowhere in sight. The man began to have a change of heart. Perhaps he had acted rashly and would live to regret what he had done. Already he missed Figaro's company. Walking to a nearby tree he hung the cage on a branch, leaving the door wide open. Then he called out to the parakeet the way he used to. Still no sight of Figaro. Dusk was descending, melting into the dark gray as the air chilled. The man felt sad and lonely.

Just as he was consoling himself over his loss, he saw a tiny object flying toward the cage. His little pet was hungry and was returning home.

The tale touched Marina to the depth of her soul; it made her think of her own son. Yo-Yo was getting older, and judging from the critical reviews she had been reading in the papers, before long, his success would be taking him away from home to perform beyond the confines of Manhattan. Sooner or later, he'd have to be evermore on his own. But, like the bird, she hoped he'd come back to the "nest." The close family cultural ties with which he had been brought up surely must have taken root. Of that she had no doubts. The publicity he was getting certainly could not change his beautiful personality and his attachment to the family.

Settling back in her chair, Marina pondered the influence exerted by critics in the making of a performer. Already she saw the importance of their role in her own son's life.

At the beginning of their careers, musicians are awed by the power of the pen. They live in fear by what may be written about their performances. One or two negative reviews and their reputations stand to suffer for years. Critics can make or break them. Eventually they learn to take things in stride, the good with the bad, but the fear is ever present. Yo-Yo learned that early on.

After one of his concerts or recitals, Yo-Yo and his mother would hop into a cab late at night and head for Times Square to pick up the next morning's newspaper editions. While the cabbie waited, they would anxiously leaf through the pages until they came to the critics' section.

On one such occasion, the review was highly favourable. The critic had lavished praises on the young cellist intimating that he was destined to become the future Pablo Casals. Elated by what they read, mother and son got into the cab and asked the driver to take them back home. When they got there, Yo-Yo handed the driver a ten-dollar bill and told him to keep the change.

Once alone, Marina turned to her son, "Yo-Yo, why did you give him so much money? Are you crazy? Five dollars would have been more than enough."

With his usual, benevolent smile, he answered, "Mom, when a person is happy he wants to share that happiness with others."

What could she say? She knew Yo-Yo was a very generous person.

At other times Marina got up at 4:00 or 5:00 in the morning and rushed out to buy newspapers so that she could read what the critics had said about Yo-Yo's performance of the previous evening. At that ungodly hour the streets were deserted, but her desire to see the reviews far outweighed the fear for her own safety despite the terrible stories she had heard about neighbourhood crimes. But as she watched newscasts of murders, muggings, vandalism, and assaults on innocent people, it dawned on her that it was foolish to risk her life. Some other way had to be found...

She knew that the occupants of the apartment below subscribed to a delivery service, which left newspapers behind the door in the early morning hours. Quietly she would creep downstairs, pick up the paper, open nervously to the review page and quickly scan the articles. Then, very carefully replacing the paper exactly the way she had found it, she ran back upstairs.

If Yo-Yo was awake, she would blurt out, "The reviews are good."

"How do you know, Mom? It's still so early."

"I just read the newspaper," she would answer in a casual manner.

"Let me see it."

"I don't have it."

Then she confessed.

As she spoke, she realized how embarrassing it would have been if the neighbour downstairs had opened the door and caught her.

Of course, she could have easily waited until later in the day to buy a newspaper; that would have been the logical thing to do. But the waiting would have been too stressful. Besides, mothers don't always follow logic when it concerns their children.

25. Rostropovich's Cello End Pin

Rostropovich, that irrepressible, critically acclaimed, Russian cellist was appearing on T.V. in a command performance. Classical music devotees sat mesmerized before their sets, watching, absorbing the tender, poignant feelings the maestro of artistic expression drew forth from his instrument. Marina was one of those viewers. As he played, she envisioned her son in his place, performing the same Haydn *Concerto in C*, wondering if her son would someday follow in Rostropovich's footsteps.

It was understandable that she should be elated when Yo-Yo informed her that the maestro was going to give two master classes at the Juilliard College School of Music, where Yo-Yo was taking lessons while studying privately with Leonard Rose.

"Are you going?" his mother asked.

"Oh, Mom, what a question. Do you think I would miss such a golden opportunity? As a matter of fact, I'm going to both sessions."

Marina was glad. The internationally renowned artist deserved this respect and reverence. A man dedicated to the ennoblement of the performing arts, he was an excellent model for young people to emulate. She thought, however, that attending one master class was sufficient. Her son thought otherwise.

Yo-Yo sat close to the stage, awed, drinking in every note, watching every movement of Rostropovich's fingering and his total control of the bowing. But there was something else that struck him, something that undoubtedly no one else had observed: the end pin on Rostropovich's cello was bent at an angle permitting the player to hold the instrument more nearly parallel to the floor. Thus held, the cello allowed him to lean back and assume a more comfortable position.

There was nothing extraordinary in that; practically every cellist has his own favourite way of positioning the instrument between his legs to get the best control. Most cellos, including Yo-Yo's, however, have a straight end pin, which forces the player to lean forward. So greatly was Yo-Yo impressed by this simple device that he asked his parents to have his own cello end pin replaced.

"Son," Dr. Ma said, "do you realize what an expense that would be for us? Eighty dollars is a lot of money to spend just for that." But the youngster pleaded and in the end had his way.

When Yo-Yo went for his lesson with Leonard Rose, the maestro noticed the change. "What's that?" he asked, pointing to the end pin with his finger.

"Oh, that?" Yo-Yo replied, surprised that the slight alteration had been noticed so quickly. "That's my new end pin. I feel much more comfortable playing this way."

Nothing more was said.

The following week, the same dialogue between teacher and student was repeated. This time, however, Mr. Rose remarked in terms that left no room for misunderstanding; "Well, I think you should go back to the original straight end pin." For Yo-Yo this was tantamount to an order.

Meanwhile, back at the Juilliard College, other students having noticed the bent end pin on Yo-Yo's cello had the same thing done to theirs. He must have had a good reason, they thought.

When Yo-Yo returned to class and the students noticed the straight end pin on his cello, they were bewildered.

Did they too make the change?

Well, let's leave that to the imagination.

26. *The Culture Crisis*

I n Paris, Hiao-Tsiun had adapted himself to French culture while still retaining Chinese ways. After settling with his family in New York City, he anticipated no serious problems for himself or for his family with a third culture. At home, the family would continue to use the Chinese language; at table they would eat essentially Chinese food; the décor of their apartment would mirror their Oriental ways.

According to traditional upbringing, the children would obey their father without question. Dr. Ma expected nothing less from Yo-Yo, who was considered an extension of his parents. How he behaved, how he was perceived outside the home was a reflection of the family's integrity.

All this was fine...at home. But in the outside world, the impressionable boy was faced with contradictory and confusing sets of values.

It was inevitable for Yo-Yo, growing up in New York City, to find himself at odds with the traditional, totally structured Chinese system in which the child submerged his individuality to authority. He was now constantly exposed to a free, American society, which glorified the inalienable rights of each individual.

Yo-Yo was born in Paris of Chinese parents and lived there till the age of seven, when the family moved to Manhattan. During the summer school vacations, he returned to France with them. As long as he was still very young and close to home, coping with cultural differences was not difficult. But as soon as he grew older and observed the behaviour of other youngsters, he became more and more aware that he was "different." Furthermore, peer pressure was intensified for him "to belong." Little by little, this pressure translated into an inner

Yo-Yo at 15.

struggle of conscience: his tri-cultural background became a paradox.

Without a doubt, he loved his father; at the same time he feared his strict discipline and unbending ways. Although Yo-Yo admired him for what he stood for, he could not always share his values. As Yo-Yo grew older, this repressed inner conflict erupted into the open. It began manifesting itself in the fifth grade, when he occasionally played hooky from classes. During his high school days, he often took long walks alone "to get away from it all."

But before reaching high school, he had to cope with another problem: boredom. His academic ability was far beyond his grade level at the Professional Children's School in Manhattan. Fortunately, this hurdle was short lived because they soon placed him in an accelerated program enabling him to graduate at the age of fifteen.

After receiving his high school diploma, he enrolled in Juilliard's College Division. The following summer, he attended Ivan Galamian's

(In deep concentration...) Caspary Hall, Rockefeller Center. Rehearsing for the Children's Orchestra Concert.

music camp at Meadowbrook, in the Adirondacks. Away from home and parental authority at last, he gave free rein to his pent-up emotions, rebelling against authority. In his own words, "he went wild," missing rehearsals, leaving his cello carelessly outside in all kinds of weather, and engaging in midnight "escapades."

Not until later, while at Juilliard College, did he realize the full impact of his actions and the danger ahead.

27. The Rebellion

Marina was deeply concerned about her teenage son; perhaps it was needless, but this was a critical period in his life. True, the Mas had been overly protective causing Yo-Yo to resent their warnings and advice.

"You worry too much," he told them, "I'm perfectly capable of taking care of myself."

"But we are living through difficult times," they would reiterate, trying to impress on him the dangers of the outside world.

Marina feared that some of Yo-Yo's peers would exert a negative influence, which might prove detrimental to him and to his career.

"You must be very careful," she warned. "Jealousy can cause great harm." She had in mind a certain cello student who had become a close friend of Yo-Yo's. "I can understand why a classmate would envy you. In his place, I would too."

Yo-Yo grimaced as his mother was speaking. Nevertheless, she continued.

"Perhaps you should consider ending the friendship."

Yo-Yo was annoyed. "Oh, Mom, you always think the worst. I'm no longer a child. I know what I'm doing."

"I'm glad you think so, but you still have a lot to learn about people."

Marina's fears were confirmed.

Yo-Yo had a friend, older than he, who had been playing cello for a longer time and had a more extensive repertoire. Nevertheless, he used to ask Yo-Yo to select the music which they played together. Thrilled that his friend relied on his judgment, Yo-Yo trusted him fully. Unfortunately, the older one was into drinking and influenced Yo-Yo into joining him and his companions in their bad habits. It was a new and exciting experience for the young prodigy. He felt more mature as he fitted in with the group. Acquiring a false I.D. card (he was still under age) enabled him to purchase alcoholic beverages and to revel in the spirit of camaraderie with the others.

At home, of course, no one ever suspected what he was up to until one Friday afternoon…

28. One Friday Afternoon

Fridays, precisely at 4:00 p.m., at the Sacred Heart School in upper Manhattan, Dr. Ma rehearsed the Children's Orchestra, which he had founded. He was preparing for the annual concert at Caspary Hall of the Rockefeller Institute. The children ranged from four to fifteen years of age. Discipline was the order of the day. Rehearsals began on time and no excuse for lateness was tolerated.

On this particular Friday, Yo-Yo did not show up even though he knew his presence was indispensable to the orchestra. The classical pieces that the children were playing needed his leadership.

Fifteen minutes went by; then thirty...

Marina, who always assisted her husband at rehearsals, was worried. It was not like her son to disappoint his father. What if he didn't show up at all? The thought alone was enough to send chills down her spine. She dreaded the scene that was sure to take place at home that evening, having no stomach for it. The hands on the clock seemed to be moving faster than usual. It was already 4:45 p.m. She kept looking at the entrance for Yo-Yo to arrive. Someone did finally appear: it was the school receptionist. She walked up to Marina with a message, "You're wanted on the phone, Mrs. Ma."

"Did they say who's calling?" Marina asked, her voice quivering.

"No. They just asked for you."

Marina's heart skipped a beat, as she hurried to the reception desk to pick up the receiver. At the other end of the line a voice asked, "Are you Mrs. Ma?" It was a student from Juilliard College. "Don't be frightened," the voice said in an almost inaudible tone, "your son has been taken to the emergency room at Roosevelt Hospital."

"*Mon Dieu!*" Marina gasped. They were the only words she could summon up; others stuck in her throat. Then, as if recovering from some kind of stupor, "What happened? Is my son all right?"

"Please calm down, Mrs. Ma. He's O.K. now. He just had too much to drink. "

Marina was stunned.

"He's still too young," the voice on the telephone volunteered, "he needs to do some growing up."

Frantic, Marina rushed out of the building without breathing a word to her husband. She hailed a taxi and within a half hour she was in the emergency room.

"He'll be all right," the doctor reassured her. "We pumped out his stomach."

Marina walked over to her son's bed and looked at him compassionately. "Yo-Yo, Yo-Yo, why, oh why?" was all she could say.

29. Saving Face

That evening Marina made up her mind to tell her husband about Yo-Yo's hospitalization; she couldn't let the matter slide by: it was too important. Besides, sooner or later, he was bound to find out; it was best for him to hear it from her. She knew her husband would be mortified by the shame Yo-Yo had brought upon the family.

She led her husband into the dining room where they would not be overheard. "I have something to tell you," she began, "but please, please, just this once, listen to me before you say anything." And she proceeded to tell him why Yo-Yo had missed the rehearsal. "He's not well, right now. Don't punish him. He has suffered enough. If you punish him, it will be worse. Much worse. But if you deal openly with the problem, he may yet mend his ways; he's still young; he'll straighten out. I know our son. I know him." And her heart pounded. Did she really know him?

For a moment her husband stood there silent, stone-like. He never thought such a thing could ever have happened.

"What do you suggest we do?" It was not like him to remain calm in circumstances such as these. But this was an entirely different emotion that he felt. Music was one thing, fatherly love was another.

"First of all," she said, "I promised Yo-Yo that I would not tell you what happened and I wouldn't want him to lose faith in me. But sooner or later you would have found out. It's best you hear the truth from me."

She went on to tell him about Yo-Yo's drinking, concocting as she went along a simple but plausible scenario. Dr. Ma was to say that as he stood on a subway platform waiting for a train, he ran into one of Yo-Yo's schoolmates and was asked, "How's Yo-Yo doing? I haven't seen him in class since he left the hospital." In talking things over with his son, Dr. Ma was to pretend that was how he learned of the emergency room episode.

Marina knew how intelligent a man her husband was, kind and affectionate; but she was also aware how easily he could become upset.

"Stay very calm," she cautioned him. "Do not punish Yo-Yo. I'll be at your side and act surprised by what you're telling him. It's the only way to deal with the problem," she concluded.

"You're right," he told her. "Friends can sometimes be your enemies. Yo-Yo has a lot to learn."

Dr. Ma took a soft approach as he went to speak to his son, appealing to reason. "Maybe you don't realize it, Yo-Yo, but I need you at rehearsals, and when you don't show up, the entire orchestra suffers. You let the children down, and that is not fair to them."

His words produced the intended effect. Yo-Yo understood the meaning of responsibility toward others. It had never been his intention to hurt anyone. It was not in his character. A confrontation was thus averted as father and son reached out to each other.

"Perhaps I've done you some wrong in drinking a glass of wine at mealtime," Dr. Ma concluded, "I may have unknowingly set a bad example for you. From now on, I'll not drink wine anymore."

The unexpected attitude of his father, the calm way in which he handled the crisis produced the desired effect on the sensitive youth. Yo-Yo had no intention of depriving his father of such a harmless pleasure.

"It's not right; it's not right at all that Daddy should punish himself because of me," Yo-Yo later told his mother.

Ridden by a sense of guilt, Yo-Yo promised that he would never again abuse alcohol. His "kicking the habit" was his way of expressing his love and admiration for his father.

Weeks later, Marina was sitting quietly in the room while Yo-Yo was practicing. Suddenly he stopped playing.

"You were right, Mom. I should have listened to you."

"Listen to me about what?" she retorted. She had no idea to what he was referring.

"Remember what you said about envy and the fellow I used to play music with?"

She remembered.

"Well, recently I learned from one of my friends that he was out to ruin my career."

It was not the moment to tell him, "I told you so." She simply said, "It was your own fault, Yo-Yo. No one should be blamed. And do you know why? Because each time after both of you had lessons with Mr. Rose, you used to say to your friend, 'Mr. Rose told me what a fine cellist you are.' You meant well in praising him. But your words gave him the wrong idea. If you had not praised him so much, maybe he would not have been so envious of you or vindictive; he would not have dreamed of putting himself in the same category as you."

She searched for an analogy.

"Suppose, just suppose that I don't speak Italian or French. How can anyone who speaks Italian or French be jealous of me? But if I spoke those two languages to perfection and another person did not, then that might be reason enough for his being envious and building up hatred for me. Without meaning to, you gave him false encouragement by inventing what Mr. Rose had told you. The student believed you because he wanted to believe he was equal to you. This was sufficient enough for him to bear you a grudge and try to undermine your ability. In making up his mind to surpass you, he pretended to be your friend and pressured you into drinking."

Yo-Yo listened without making reply. Then he positioned his bow and resumed his practice.

30. Illustrious "Chain Links"

H ad Yo-Yo's grandmother not been so persistent about her daughter-in-law's having another child, who knows? Yo-Yo may have never been born. Poor old woman! She did not live long enough to see her grandson become one of the world's great cellists. After an illness of four months, she died precisely on his first birthday.

Marina's life nor her husband's had ever been easy. She had given up her singing career to raise their two children. During moments of tranquillity, she wondered whether she too could have had a successful career, yet she never regretted the sacrifice.

As a caring mother, she shared the challenges facing her son during his growing years. Yo-Yo did not always adhere to the expected code of behaviour, but through parental guidance and self-examination, he finally came to the realization that his teenage misdeeds had to come to an end.

Several luminaries in the field of music, who had inspired, tutored or influenced Yo-Yo are now dead, but the chain-links that helped catapult him to success will not be forgotten. Janos Scholz,[10] who had accepted the young prodigy as his private pupil on the recommendation of Arthur Grumiaux, the Belgian violinist, gave Yo-Yo free lessons for two years. It is understandable that both teacher and pupil were deeply moved at their separation, for the time had come for Yo-Yo to attend Juilliard College and to begin studying with Leonard Rose.

---

10. Janos Scholz, died on 3 June 1993.

Alexander Schneider,[11] had introduced Yo-Yo to Pablo Casals,[12] who in turn brought him to the attention of Leonard Bernstein,[13] and Leonard Rose,[14] his principal cello teacher, who had taught his young student "to be at one" with his instrument.

In an interview with Howard Reich, Yo-Yo quoted the advice given him by Mr. Rose, whom he had always considered his close friend and mentor, "When you play, you must feel as though the instrument is part of your body, the strings are your voice, and the cello is your lungs."

It is said that musicians are born and that talents are made. The truism clearly applies to Yo-Yo. Thanks to the family into which he was born, he was destined to shine from the very beginning. The music that flows from his cello is the voice of his soul; the language it speaks is the universal language understood by the mind and felt by the heart. Isaac Stern, who first heard Yo-Yo play at the age of five and who invited him in later years to become a regular participant in the now well known chamber music ensemble, "Isaac Stern and Friends," maintained that one had "to have the bow arm be the guide, but to let his ears become the motivation factor." Yo-Yo learned to do just that.

In pleasing his own ear, Yo-Yo has also succeeded in pleasing the ear of his listeners, who, as Marina expressed in her own simple way, interact with him. "The audience is one with him; when he breathes, the audience also breathes; when he stops, the audience also stops. As Yo-Yo becomes absorbed in his music, so does the audience. It isn't how far the audience takes him, but how far he takes the audience with his playing. It is that special, magic moment when artist and audience are fused into one. Ever since childhood, Yo-Yo has had this power to attract people and move them. He is happy when others share his feelings for music and he revels in that moment of ecstasy

---

11. Alexander Schneider, died on 2 February 1993.
12. Pablo Casals, died on 22 October 1973.
13. Leonard Bernstein, died on 14 October 1990.
14. Leonard Rose, died on 16 November 1984.

when the audience forgets itself and is transported by the sheer beauty of sound. For Yo-Yo has that consummate gift to penetrate the mind and the heart of the composer and transmit that feeling to the audience, who is in total harmony with him."

Music critics have not failed to acknowledge this audience reaction. William Mootz wrote:

> This youthful Chinese-American galloped on stage with a smile that could have melted icebergs. Before he played a note, he had his audience captivated. When he drew his bow across his instrument a few minutes later, he had us all mesmerized.[15]

Did Marina, who had trained as an opera singer, coach her son on his stage presence? She denied it. Nevertheless, his body movements suggest "stage" directions. She added that they were natural with Yo-Yo; he was always a keen observer. "The movements are not rehearsed nor are they mere frills; in his case, they help to enhance his technique. If an opera singer wants to project her voice far," she explained, "accompanying gestures help her reach the audience, 'drawing' it into the act. That is precisely the point of a performer: he 'pulls in' the public. With his particular technique and spontaneous movements, Yo-Yo's cello projects its 'voice' far. The audience, captivated, is moved emotionally."

On stage, Yo-Yo offers joy, excitement and rapture, which linger long after the performance has ended. His manner of playing bonds him to the spectators and a spiritual communion takes place "lifting them onto the stage and onto him." Were this not so, one could easily listen to his recordings.

Yo-Yo often asked his mother to listen to two or three different interpretations of a musical composition.

"Yo-Yo, I know next to nothing about cellos; you know that."

"Yes, but you know about singing. Tell me which version you like best."

---

15. *The Courier Journal*, Louisville, Kentucky, 2 February 1974.

Even after Yo-Yo had a measure of fame, he wanted to hear what his father
thought of his performance.

Whichever one she chose, he would ask her to justify her
preference.

"It's simple. I like simple things," she'd answer.

He would then practice that rendition.

His mother worried about her answer. "Had I chosen the wrong
version, what effect would it have had on his career? That has always
been on my conscience."

Her husband also felt the onus of making decisions for Yo-Yo. He
constantly preached, "Observe the minutest details; concentrate and
concentrate."

With his photographic mind, Yo-Yo took everything in at a
glance," Marina reflected. "Had he chosen to be an artist instead of a

musician, he would have been an outstanding one because he paid attention to every little detail."

Through it all, even after gaining a measure of fame, Yo-Yo still turned to his parents for their reaction to his performances. They were honest with him and he respected their judgment with continued faith. He has never forgotten their parental advice to listen to his cello for tone, colour and texture, in the same way as he used to listen to his mother's voice when she sang for him. When performing, he shuts his eyes and tilts his head backwards, his jet black hair punctuating his precise body movements. He becomes one with the composer and the composition. The composer's creation is then heard not only through the lyric flow of Yo-Yo's playing but also through the "voice" of his cello.

His wild experience at Galamian's music camp over, Yo-Yo realized that, besides music, he needed something more to round out his life. He registered at Columbia University to remain close to home, and continued his lessons with Mr. Rose. After one semester at Columbia University, he became disenchanted with his studies and, unknown to his parents, dropped out to return full-time to Juilliard College.

Now, approaching the age of seventeen, he found himself at a crossroads. Should he devote himself wholly to a musical career or broaden his academic knowledge? He opted to do both by enrolling at Harvard University — no ordinary feat even for someone of Yo-Yo's intellectual prowess. The Chinese discipline against which he had rebelled in the past played no small part in his decision. More than that, his natural curiosity made him thirst for knowledge.

Harvard University opened a wide door. Now he had the possibility to search freely for the meaning of life beyond music. There Yo-Yo learned that, in music, he could give equal importance to an intellectual approach without subordinating the spontaneity of an intuitive interpretation.

Yo-Yo is a superstar now. His achievements, however, did not result without hard, sustained work. He plays effortlessly, without thinking of notes. Undoubtedly, his mastery of Bach *études* at an early age, which his father insisted that he learn, contributed greatly to the technique which he has developed.

Juilliard Pre–College Orchestra

Saturday Afternoon, May 22, 1971, at 3:00

Isaiah Jackson, *Conductor*

MOZART	Overture to "The Magic Flute"
HAYDN	Symphony No. 99 in E-flat major

Adagio; Vivace assai
Adagio
Menuetto: Allegretto
Finale: Vivace

INTERMISSION

SAINT-SAËNS	Concerto No. 1 in A minor for Cello and Orchestra, Opus 33

Allegro non troppo
Allegretto con moto
Allegro non troppo; Un peu moins vite

YO-YO MA, *Cello*

RAVEL	"Mother Goose" Suite

"The Pavane of the Sleeping Beauty"
"Hop-o' My Thumb"
"Laideronnette, Empress of the Pagodas"
"Conversation of Beauty and the Beast"
"The Fairy Garden"

**This program is made possible with the support of
The New York State Council on the Arts.**

The taking of photographs and the use of recording equipment are not allowed in this auditorium.
Members of the audience who must leave the auditorium before the end of the
concert are earnestly requested to do so between numbers, not during the performance.

A

ISAIAH JACKSON was born in Richmond, Virginia, where he began piano study at the age of four and clarinet study at the age of nine. Following graduation from The Putney School in Vermont, where he did considerable work with the orchestra and chorus, he entered Harvard University and majored in Russian history and literature, receiving his Bachelor of Arts degree *cum laude* in 1966. However, Mr. Jackson continued his musical activities at Harvard and conducted full productions of such works as *Don Giovanni, Così fan tutte* and *The Beggar's Opera*. During his senior year at Harvard, he also held the post of Music Director of the Bach Society Orchestra. Mr. Jackson did his graduate work at Stanford University and was appointed Assistant Conductor of the Stanford Symphony Orchestra. He came to The Juilliard School in 1968 as a candidate for the Doctor of Musical Arts degree in the class of Jean Morel. During his first year in New York, Mr. Jackson founded The New Amsterdam Chamber Orchestra, which has performed throughout the New York Metropolitan area and Connecticut. In the spring of 1969 he was appointed Music Director of the Youth Symphony Orchestra of New York and conductor of the Juilliard Pre-College Orchestra. Last summer he accepted a conducting fellowship at the Berkshire Festival, summer home of the Boston Symphony Orchestra. This fall Mr. Jackson was named Assistant Conductor of the American Symphony Orchestra under Leopold Stokowski and Associate Conductor of the American Ballet Company.

YO-YO MA was born in Paris, France, in 1955 to a family with a long and distinguished tradition in music. He began studying the cello with his father, Dr. Hiao-Tsiun Ma, and Madame Michele Lepinte at the age of four and gave his first recital two years later at the Institute of Art and Archeology at the University of Paris, accompanied by his sister, four years his senior. He gave his second recital just before his sixth birthday at Nazareth College in Rochester, New York. Mr. Ma moved to New York with his family in 1962 and completed his elementary schooling at the École Française and Trinity School. In 1964 he participated in a benefit concert for the École Française in Carnegie Hall. In 1968 he entered the Professional Children's School, from which he will graduate this June. Mr. Ma has given many recitals in this country and in Europe. In 1968 he was soloist with the San Francisco Little Symphony performing the Saint-Saëns Cello Concerto No. 1, and was invited to return in 1970 to perform the work with the San Francisco Symphony, Seiji Ozawa conducting. In 1969, Sol Hurok Management added him to its list of artists. This season Mr. Ma was invited to give a recital at the United Nations. In March he performed Tchaikovsky's *Rococo Variations* with the Harvard-Radcliffe Orchestra and gave a recital at Radcliffe College later that month. On May 6, Mr. Ma made his official New York debut in Carnegie Recital Hall. Mr. Ma entered the Juilliard Pre-College Division in 1964 and has studied jointly with Leonard Rose and Channing Robbins since that time.

JUILLIARD PRE-COLLEGE ORCHESTRA PERSONNEL

VIOLIN
Amy Barlowe
Conrad Biel
Laurie Carney
Joseph Chen
Min-Yen Chien
Hanwon Choi
Young Sun Choi
Brian Dembow
Inez Hassman
William Hayden
Paul Kantor
Hae Kyoung Kim
Marjorie Kransberg
Ellen Mellow
David Pesetsky
Aida Philibosian
Jeffrey Puccio
Michael Rosenbloom
Carl Rosoff
Jonathan Schreiber
Susan Seymour
Do-Yeong Shin
Marc Silberger
Pamela Sixfin
Sharon Smith
Gunar Upelnieks
Helaina Zades

VIOLA
Marin Alsop
Edward Deitch
Lawrence Dutton
Mark Kaplan

Sandra Kurtis
Sung Ju Lee
Joel Pitchon
Gayle Schechtman
Adam Silk
Yang-Chun Yi

CELLO
Marianne Chen
Pierre Djokic
Steven Finnerty
Gary Fitzgerald
Mary Greenblatt
Bonnie Hartman
Ellen Levy
Yo-Yo Ma
Hilda Movsessian
Robert Osman
John Reed

DOUBLE BASS
Joseph Bongiorno
Judith Sugarman

FLUTE
Stephen Baum
Patricia Noordsij
Jan Reuter

OBOE
Lester Forest
Susan Gellert
Arnold Greenwich

CLARINET
Donald Lurye
Karen Rockwell

BASSOON
Bruce Adolphe
Ethan Bauch
Larry Turyn

HORN
Theodore Freed
Stephen Multer

TRUMPET
Anthony Gonzalez
Brian King

TROMBONE
Michael Gisser
Howard Prince

TUBA
Paul Coleman

PERCUSSION
Larry Balin
Scott Bleaken
David Fein
Martin Kluger

HARP
Carol Emanuel
Rachel Van Voorhees

B

Yo-Yo's selection as the sole recipient of the prestigious Avery Fisher Prize in 1978, his subsequent honorary degrees from Harvard, Yale and other universities, and his appearances as guest artist with major orchestras, including the New York Philharmonic, the Chicago Symphony, the Boston and Philadelphia Orchestras, the Los Angeles Philharmonic, and the Chamber Music Society of Lincoln Center in the United States and with the English Chamber Orchestra, the Berlin Philharmonic, the Royal Philharmonic, the Orchestre Nationale de France, the Israel Philharmonic, and the Vienna Philharmonic overseas attest to the prominence he enjoys in classical music. Most of all, his prankish sense of humour, his sparkling personality, his generosity and his love "to make music" for audiences the world over continue to endear him to all.

 *Epilogue*

"I guess I've told you enough about Yo-Yo's early years, Dr. Rallo," Marina concluded as our conversation was ending. "Time and distance have blurred many details. Yo-Yo is now a public figure; his art will be judged by music critics and by the vast following he has. As for his private life, that's exactly how it should remain: private."

She raised her eyes to glance at the clock.

"In a little while, it'll be time to feed my husband. Would you like a cup of tea?"

I nodded.

"I remember. You like it very light, Chinese style."

She looked in the direction of her husband's bedroom. "He'll never go back to Ormesson," she sighed and a furtive tear clouded her eyes; "he had so much looked forward to that." Then, as if to find some sort of consolation, she added, "At least he knows I'm here with him, as I've been throughout our lives. But I must tell you something. Sometimes my husband asks, 'Do you really want to stay here with me? I'm a lot of trouble to you.'"

"Of course I want to stay here and take care of you, where else should I want to be? Then a little sad smile forms on the corner of his lips. You know, in spite of his illness, I am sure he is at peace with himself. And his sense of humour is still with him."

Once, at the hospital, a nurse asked him, "How many children do you have, Dr. Ma?"

"Six," he quickly replied, emphasizing the number six.

Marina, who was standing by, thought he was losing his memory.

"Daddy," she said in her affectionate way, "you know you don't have six children."

He blinked his eyes and nodded his head in affirmation.

"Very well, then, tell me their names."

"Yeou-Cheng," he began.

"And the second child?"

"Yo-Yo."

"And the third?"

Marina thought she had trapped him.

"Ping-Li."

"And the fourth?"

"Ping-Lai."

"And the fifth?"

"Ping-Chou."

"And the sixth?"

"Ping-Lan."

His answers rolled off his tongue in Chinese, one after the other.

Amazed, Marina said, "Now, what are you saying? Ping-Li and Ping-Lai are Yeou-Cheng's children, and Ping-Chou and Ping-Lan are Yo-Yo's children. You thought you could fool me. That's smart of you. Very smart. You took your grandchildren and made them your own."

"You see, Dr. Rallo, my husband can still find humour in life. I must confess, though, at times he does get things mixed up and doesn't recognize people; he doesn't even know where he is." Pathos stuck in her voice.

She poured me a cup of jasmine tea and poured one for herself.

In spite of her husband's condition, life remains beautiful for Marina. She considers herself fortunate. While reliving her past, however, her focus is on the future.

Yeou-Cheng has combined her pediatric practice with a musical career. Besides raising two children, Daniel and Laura, she and her husband, Michael Dadap, a classical guitarist, give recitals and concerts. The Children's Orchestra, founded by Dr. Ma, is now under their capable direction.

Yo-Yo is happily married to the former Jill Hornor, a Harvard Professor of German. Nowadays he has so many commitments in the United States and abroad that little time is left to be with his family. Fortunately, Jill is a wonderful wife and mother. She understands, and

(From left to right) Michael Dadap, Marina holding Daniel, Dr. Hiao-Tsiun Ma holding Laura, and Yeou-Cheng.

(From left to right) Yo-Yo and family: Nicholas, Jill and Emily in Daddy's lap.

Yo-Yo and Jill (before their wedding).

(From left to right) Laura, Michael, Yeou-Cheng and Daniel.

looks forward eagerly to the month of July when Yo-Yo shuts out the world for thirty-one days of peace and quiet with her and their two lively but adorable children, Nicholas and Emily.

From his sick bed, Hiao-Tsiun Ma contemplates the photos of his grandchildren hanging on one wall of his bedroom. His mind, very much alert, perhaps wonders which one of them will be the next child prodigy. Soft music, Mozart and Bach, comes through the door, a fitting background for his dreams.[16]

As I listen silently to Marina Ma's parting thoughts, I fully understand what she means by "love of family." And I call to mind the time Yo-Yo gave a concert at the Van Wezel Hall in Sarasota, Florida.

Unknown to Yo-Yo, my wife and I were in the audience. We had not seen one another for several years. Great was his surprise to find us backstage, waiting in line to congratulate him on his performance. As soon as he caught sight of us, he worked his way through a line of admirers and in his usual natural, unpretentious manner led us directly to his dressing room. There he introduced us to Emanuel Ax, his celebrated piano collaborator.

"I already seem to know them," Mr. Ax said to Yo-Yo. "You've often spoken about them."

My wife and I did not want to tarry too long, having no desire to deprive his many admirers from getting his autograph, so we made excuses to take leave.

"Wait. Just a moment," Yo-Yo said. "I have something to show you."

There on a table was his priceless 1712 Stradivari, formerly in Jacqueline Du Pré's possession. We thought he was going to tell us about the rare instrument, but, to our surprise, he opened the case and with a broad, fatherly grin that lit up his entire face, he pointed to photographs of his two children: Nicholas and Emily. "I can't be with them often," he said, "but they go with me wherever I go."

While I looked at the tender faces in the two photos, the image of another boy — now their father — flashed across my mind, and I

---

16. He died peacefully in bed on Wednesday, 28 August 1991.

Mother and son (1994).

couldn't help recalling what had happened at the École Française, a long time ago, precisely in 1966 when Yo-Yo was eleven years old. He was sent to my office for some minor infraction of school regulations, the nature of which I do not recall. In the course of my "lecturing" to him about responsibility, I saw his eyes welling up with tears from embarrassment. "Yo-Yo," I remember saying, "I can well understand what's going through your mind; I, too, am the product of different cultures. But in your case, much more is expected of you. You were not born to be like most others. You were destined to make a difference in the music world. You are going to be famous. You are like a royal person, who must answer to the public for his behaviour. Your life does not belong to you alone; it belongs to the world. This is the destiny to which you were born. The very joy and delight which we derive from your music exacts a heavy price from you."

As I prepared to bid Mrs. Ma good-bye, I repeated this episode to her. She looked at me philosophically. "Time," she said, "can wound, but it can also heal." To which, borrowing a verse from the poet, Lillian Everts,[17] I added: "Time is more than a matter of hands upon a clock." She nodded in agreement, confident that the bow "with a voice" will continue to sing.

*   *   *

In telling her story of Yo-Yo's early years, Marina hopes that, in reading the account, other young people may be inspired by it. Working together with those who love them, they may realize that life is a struggle uphill, and that pain is part of growing up. "They should bear in mind," she told me, "that love is the sustaining force that keeps a family together. Bridges are there to help us get across when obstacles bar the way."

17. Lillian Everts, Farrar, Straus and Cudahy, *Journey to the Future* (New York, 1955).

Appendices

Appendix One
What the Critics Have Said

"He exhibited phenomenal precision and unbelievable power of memory and interpretation." Sister Rose Alice, Professor in charge, Music Department, Nazareth College

The Gleaner

"Child prodigy Yo-Yo Ma, 7-year old cellist, who is accompanied on the piano by his 11-year old sister, thrills the multitude at the Armory gathered to hear the special benefit show to promote the building of a National Cultural Center here."

The Evening Star (30 November 1962).

"I want to tell you on behalf of the National Cultural Center how very much we appreciated your appearing on the telecast "The American Pageant of the Arts". Many people from all over the United States have told me that they enjoyed your charming performance tremendously ..."

Roger L. Stevens, in a letter to Yo-Yo and Yeou-Cheng (9 December 1962).

"Poise and assurance — Yo-Yo Ma, the conductor's 9-year-old son, a cellist, then joined his 12-year-old sister Yeou-Cheng to play Sammartini's *G Major Cello Sonata*. This is no children's piece, nor did they play it like children. The performance had assurance, poise and full measure of delicate musicality."

New York Times (18 December 1964, after the Carnegie Hall Program).

"The program, for the WCBS-TV, *GATEWAY*, will be repeated Saturday, 24 August, at 4:00 p.m. on Channel 2 in colour. This was one of our best programs of the series and I am glad we have the chance to air it again."

Bill Bryan, Producer and Director (12 August 1968).

"Yo-Yo Ma, a *protégé* of Pablo Casals, is nothing short of a full-fledged virtuoso of his instrument. He deserves bouquets not only for an absolutely flawless technique, this including impeccable intonation, but for a mature musicality which is positively staggering."

Arthur Bloomfield, *San Francisco Examiner* (28 October 1968).

"On the first of the San Francisco Art Commission's Little Symphony Concerts in the Presentation Theatre, conducted by Paul Freeman, young Ma breezed through with the greatest of ease and a stylishness that would be admired in a first-rate soloist of twice his years."

Robert Commanday, San Francisco Chronicle (29 October 1968).

"In the work performed by Yo-Yo Ma [Concerto in D for Cello and Orchestra] we valued both the composer [Edouard Lalo] and the interpreter. For his part [Yo-Yo Ma], the young Chinese cellist, with poetic sensitivity, with the magic world of his exceptional talent, with his musical naturalness, with his absolute mastery of his instrument, with pure fingering mechanism and with his handling of the bow, may be compared to such old masters as Pablo Casals, Fournier, Piatigorsky, Rostropovich, and Zara Nelsova....His art is indeed supreme."

Rházes Hernández Lopez, El Nacional — Caracas.

"If this boy [Yo-Yo] doesn't go down as one of the greatest cellists alive, then I don't know anything about the cello."

Leonard Rose, Denver Post.

"Yo-Yo is only 13, but already an almost surrealistically talented kid. His playing is so aristocratic, so knowing, so natural, so nimbly adaptable to the changing moods and rhythmic demands of the score, that one keeps thinking one's glasses must be on wrong and it's really a grown-up, not just a little fellow in the smallest white tie and tails you ever saw, up there on the podium."

Arthur Bloomfield, San Franscisco Examiner, (5 March 1970).

"And yesterday afternoon a Seattle audience was treated to a momentous occasion when 16-year-old Yo-Yo Ma played Antonin Dvorak's Concerto for Cello and Orchestra in B-minor, Opus 104, at the Opera House. It was exciting, indeed.
"All in all this intense young man is a cellist to watch. He knows his instrument to the ultimate and thus can exploit the flourishes of the Dvorak to the fullest. The audience yesterday afternoon gave him a standing ovation. He deserved nothing less, especially after the last two movements. The first was dramatic.... But the last two...awesome."

Rolf Stromberg, The Post-Intelliger (2 October 1972).

"Last fall [Yo-Yo] appeared in Carnegie Hall and came off as the toast of the critics.... He was a full-fledged prodigy, having begun the cello when he was 4, and is emerging in his own unorthodox way as a classical musical superstar."

John Christensen, *Louisville Times.*

Appendix Two
Yo-Yo Ma — From the Cradle to Harvard:
A Profile

1955   Born in Paris, France, 7 October 1955.

Education

1962–1963   Studied privately with father.

1963–1965   Attended the Trent School in New York City.

1965–1967   Attended the École Française in New York.
                Took courses at Juilliard's Pre-College.

1967–1968   Attended Trinity School in New York.

1968–1970   Attended Professional Children's School in New York.
                Graduated at the age of 15.
                Attended Gamalian's Summer Camp for String Players.

1970–1971   Attended Juilliard's College Division.

1971–1972   Attended Columbia University (One semester); Juilliard.

1971–1974   Marlboro Festival in Vermont (Summers).

1972–1976   Attended Harvard University; graduated with a B.A. in the
                Humanities.

Highlights of Musical Performances

1959   At age four, chose the cello as his musical instrument; started
                studying with his father, then with Mme. Michèle Lepinte.

1961   19 June, First Recital at the Institut d'Art et d'Archéologie de
                l'Université de Paris. Played the *Concertine in A Major* by
                Bréval and the *Prélude* from the Second Suite for unaccom-
                panied cello by J.S. Bach. Yeou-Cheng was the accompanist at
                the piano.
                Second Recital before his sixth birthday at Nazareth College,
                Rochester, New York, with Yeou-Cheng at the piano. Piano
                selections from Bach, Handel, Haydn, Mozart, and Beethoven.
                Yo-Yo played also Bach *Suite No. 3* for cello.

1962	11–12 January, together with his sister, presented by Saul Caston, Symphonic Concerts for Students, Denver, Colorado.
	29 November, introduced with Yeou-Cheng by Pablo Casals in a closed circuit telecast, "The American Pageant of the Arts," in Washington, D.C. Gala Benefit Concert at the Washington Armory, Leonard Bernstein, M. C.
1962–1964	Studied with Janos Scholz.
1964	29 November, appeared with Yeou-Cheng on the Johnny Carson Show.
	17 December, benefit Concert for the École Française, in Carnegie Hall.
	17 February, performed Saint-Saëns' *Concerto No. 1*, with the Doctors' Symphonic Orchestra in New York, under the Direction of Henry Block.
	Studied at Juilliard School of Music with Leonard Rose.
	2 December, introduced by Leonard Rose: CBS *GATEWAY* Program.
1968	24 August, repetition of the *GATEWAY* Program, in colour, WCBS-TV, Channel 2. Soloist with the San Francisco *Little Symphony*, Saint-Saëns' Cello *Concert No. 1*.
1969	Under Sol Hurok Management.
1970	Soloist with the San Francisco Symphony. Violoncello Recital for the United Nations Staff Day, 11 September. Yeou-Cheng at the piano.
1973	Met Emanuel Ax at Marlboro, with whom he performs regularly.
1978	Sole winner of the prestigious Avery Fisher Award.